JESUS
MY ROLE MODEL

The Life of Jesus: A Path to Follow from Birth to Ascension

Harrison S. Mungal, PhD., Psy.D.

Jesus My Role Model

Copyright © 2024 Harrison S. Mungal

All rights reserved. Neither this publication nor any part of this publication may be reproduced or transmitted in any form or by any means, electronic or mechanical, including photocopying, recording or any information storage and retrieval system, without permission in writing from the author.

Unless otherwise identified, Scripture quotations are from New King James Version of the Bible.

Contact author via email:
info@harrisonmungal.com
info@agetoage.ca
www.agetoage.ca
www.harrisonmungal.com
www.harrisonmungalbooks.com
Facebook: Harrison Mungal
Twitter: AgeToAgeInc1
LinkedIn: Harrison Mungal, Ph.D., PsyD
YouTube: Harrison Mungal
Phone: 905-533-1334

ABOUT *the* AUTHOR

Harrison Sharma Mungal, BTh, MCC, MSW, PhD, PsyD

Dr. Mungal is a devoted therapist with a background in mental health and clinical psychology, driven by a genuine passion for life and the well-being of those under his care. With an impressive literary portfolio comprising over 40 books and a seasoned public speaking career that has reached audiences in over 42 nations, he brings a wealth of knowledge and skills to his practice.

Alongside his professional accomplishments, Dr. Mungal places a high value on family, with a successful marriage of over 34 years, seven children, and multiple grandchildren. In addition to his clinical practice, Dr. Mungal and his wife have played pivotal roles in church planting, pastoral ministry, and missionary work, even during the challenging times of the Cold War in Croatia from 1994-1997. They have nurtured congregations, established churches, and served as missionaries, demonstrating a deep commitment to spreading the gospel. Their dedication extended to running a Bible college, Metro Bible College, for over a decade before transitioning into mental health and addictions counselling.

Dr. Mungal is widely respected for his unique ability to blend biblical principles with scientific insights, adding a distinctive "psychology twist" to his therapeutic approach. He explained God made us Body, Soul (mind, will and emotions) and Spirit. As much as people need support physically and spiritually, "the soul is where people are wounded and is in need of healing." His expertise has been sought after by various media outlets, including appearances on television programs including 700 Clubs Canada and 100 Huntly St. He has also been invited to speak at prestigious institutions such as the Attorney General of Canada, police departments, hospitals, community agencies, and churches. His contributions have earned him accolades and recognition from local authorities, police departments, mayors, community leaders, and countless families.

With over 21 years of experience in mental health, psychiatry, and psychology, coupled with over four decades dedicated to teaching and preaching the gospel, Dr. Mungal possesses a wealth of expertise in both fields. His educational background is equally impressive, with a Christian Leadership Certificate, a Ministerial Diploma from two years of Bible College, a bachelor's degree in Theology, two master's degrees (in Counselling and Social Work), and two doctorate degrees (in Social Work and Clinical Psychology).

In summary, Dr. Mungal's journey is a testament to his unwavering commitment to serving others, integrating his faith with his professional expertise to make a positive impact in the lives of countless individuals, couples, and families. His multifaceted career reflects a deep sense of purpose and a profound dedication to promoting holistic healing and spiritual growth.

TABLE of CONTENT

INTRODUCTION...7
MY ROLE MODEL..11
MY FRIEND 21
GOD'S PLAN 25
MY SAVIOUR 29
THE INCARNATION..41
GOD CLOTHED HIMSELF 51
THE HUMANITY SIDE..71
THE EARTH WALK 85
IN THE GARDEN 93
THE TRIAL..101
THE CRUCIFIXION 113
THE CROSS...135
HELL 159
JESUS IS ALIVE!..173

HEAVEN 183
THE COMMISSION 193
CONCLUSION 205

INTRODUCTION

Welcome to a journey that delves into the heart of one of the most compelling and transformative figures in history: Jesus Christ. As you embark on this exploration, you'll uncover the many layers of Jesus' life and teachings, each offering profound insights and timeless lessons. Through this narrative, we will navigate through the multifaceted dimensions of Jesus' existence—from His divine nature to His deeply human experiences, from His earthly ministry to His heavenly promises.

At the core of this journey, you will discover why Jesus is the ultimate role model. His life is a testament to humility, compassion, and unwavering integrity. As we explore His actions and teachings, you'll see how His example can guide us in our own lives, helping us to navigate challenges, show kindness to others, and live with purpose.

We'll dive into the personal aspect of Jesus as a friend. You'll learn how Jesus' deep empathy, unconditional love, and steadfast loyalty make Him the friend we all long for—a companion who understands our struggles and stands by us through thick and thin.

You'll gain a clearer understanding of the divine plan that Jesus came to fulfill. This part of our journey will reveal the intricacies of

God's grand design, a plan that offers hope and redemption to all of humanity. You'll see how Jesus' life and mission fit into this broader narrative, providing a sense of purpose and direction.

Explore the profound concept of Jesus as our Savior. You'll come to understand the significance of His sacrifice on the cross and the hope it brings for redemption and eternal life. This segment will illuminate the depth of Jesus' love and the lengths He went to ensure our salvation.

We will delve into the mystery of the incarnation, where God took on human form in Jesus. This remarkable event bridges the divine and the human, showing us that God is not distant but deeply involved in our lives. You'll learn how this unique aspect of Jesus' identity brings God closer to us.

Explore the significance of Jesus being God in human form. You'll discover how this extraordinary union of divine and human nature allowed Jesus to experience life as we do, offering us a profound connection with the divine.

You'll see Jesus through the lens of His humanity, understanding His joys, sorrows, and struggles. This exploration will show you a relatable figure who faced life's challenges with grace and courage, providing a model for how we can navigate our own lives.

We will walk alongside Jesus through His earthly ministry, witnessing His teachings, miracles, and acts of compassion. You'll learn how His actions and words offer timeless lessons on living a life of purpose, service, and love.

You'll gain a deeper understanding of Jesus' humanity through His agonizing prayer in the Garden of Gethsemane. This poignant moment reveals His vulnerability and resolve, teaching us about the power of surrender and faith in the face of overwhelming challenges.

We will examine the events leading up to Jesus' crucifixion, highlighting the injustice and suffering He endured. You'll learn how

Jesus' response to His trial and persecution exemplifies strength, forgiveness, and unshakable commitment to His mission.

Witness the profound sacrifice of Jesus on the cross. You'll explore the significance of His death, the love that drove Him to give His life, and the redemption that His sacrifice brings to all who believe.

You'll learn about the personal impact of Jesus' crucifixion. This segment will show how His sacrifice offers forgiveness, healing, and a new beginning, transforming our lives and opening the way to a relationship with God.

Discover what happened when Jesus descended into Hell, conquering death and sin. This victory assures us that evil does not have the final say and offers us hope for eternal life.

Celebrate the resurrection of Jesus, the cornerstone of Christian faith. You'll explore the evidence and significance of His triumph over death, affirming the hope and new life that His resurrection brings.

We will explore the promise of heaven, a place of eternal joy and peace. This hope inspires us to live with a future perspective, looking forward to a time when we will be with Jesus forever in a place free from pain and suffering.

Finally, you'll learn about Jesus' great commission to spread His message to all corners of the earth. This call to action challenges us to share the love and hope of Jesus with others, making His teachings a living reality in the world today.

As we journey through these themes, you will come to see why Jesus is not just a historical figure but a living role model, friend, and Savior. His life and teachings offer us a blueprint for living with purpose, love, and hope, guiding us toward a deeper relationship with God and a life of meaningful impact.

Embark on this journey with an open heart and mind, and allow the story of Jesus to transform you, as it has transformed countless lives throughout history.

My *role* Model

Growing up, I always admired those who stood out as role models—people whose lives seemed to embody qualities I aspired to emulate. Among them, none has captured my heart and mind more profoundly than Jesus Christ. He isn't just a historical figure or a distant theological concept to me; He's my ultimate role model, a beacon of love, compassion, and unwavering faith.

From the earliest stories I heard about Jesus, His life was marked by acts of kindness and teachings that challenged societal norms with love and grace. I remember learning about how He healed the sick, comforted the broken-hearted, and stood up for the marginalized. These stories weren't just tales of the past; they resonated deeply within me, igniting a desire to follow in His footsteps.

As I grew older and delved deeper into the Scriptures, I discovered that Jesus wasn't just a moral exemplar but the embodiment of divine truth and love. His teachings, like the Sermon on the Mount, where He spoke of humility, mercy, and peacemaking, became my compass for navigating life's complexities. I found myself drawn to His radical inclusivity and His call to love even those who opposed Him—an

MY ROLE MODEL

invitation to transcend mere tolerance and embrace genuine, transformative love.

What sets Jesus apart as my role model isn't just His teachings or miraculous deeds; it's the profound impact He continues to have on countless lives throughout history and into the present day. His sacrificial death on the cross, a selfless act of love to redeem humanity, stands as the ultimate testament to His character. The humility and obedience He displayed in facing unimaginable suffering inspire me to face my own challenges with courage and faith.

In a world often marked by division, strife, and uncertainty, Jesus remains a constant source of hope and renewal. His life serves as a blueprint for how to navigate the complexities of relationships, ethics, and personal growth with integrity and compassion. As I embark on my own journey of faith and discipleship, I find myself continually drawn to Jesus—the ultimate role model whose life and teachings transcend time and culture, offering timeless wisdom and boundless grace to all who seek it.

To me, a role model is someone who embodies qualities and values that I admire and strive to emulate in my own life. They are not just famous figures or celebrities but individuals who demonstrate integrity, kindness, resilience, and compassion in their everyday actions. A role model can be a parent, a teacher, a mentor, or even a friend whose character and choices inspire me to be a better person.

One of the key roles of a role model is to set a positive example through their words and deeds. They lead by showing how to navigate challenges with grace and perseverance. Growing up, I looked up to my grandmother as a role model. She was a woman of few words but immense integrity. Her work ethics to raise 11 children after my grandfather past away, her honesty, and unwavering commitment to her family left a lasting impression on me. Whenever I faced a difficult decision or felt uncertain, I would think about how she would approach the situation with wisdom and courage.

Responsibility is another important aspect of being a role model. Those who hold this position understand that their actions can influence others, especially young people, and they take this influence seriously. They strive to be positive influences, knowing that others may look to them for guidance and inspiration. This responsibility extends beyond personal achievements to how they treat others, handle adversity, and contribute to their communities.

A role model also serves as a mentor, offering guidance and support to those who seek their wisdom. They may not always have all the answers, but their willingness to listen, share their experiences, and offer encouragement can make a significant difference in someone's life. I have been fortunate to have mentors like my parents who believed in me, challenged me to grow, and helped me navigate career decisions and personal challenges. Their belief in my potential and their guidance shaped my path and inspired me to pay it forward by being a role model to others.

Ultimately, the impact of a role model goes beyond individual achievements or accolades. It is about leaving a legacy of kindness, integrity, and compassion that continues to ripple through generations. As I reflect on the role models in my life, I am reminded of the power of their influence and the responsibility that comes with being someone others look up to. Whether through small acts of kindness or larger gestures of leadership, each of us has the opportunity to be a positive role model and make a difference in the lives of those around us.

Jesus was not just a teacher; He was a revolutionary. His passion for His mission was evident in every word He spoke and every action He took. I remember reading about how He fearlessly confronted injustice and hypocrisy, and how His teachings resonated with authenticity and

MY ROLE MODEL

love. It wasn't just what He said, but the way He lived His life that inspired countless people then and continues to inspire me today.

One of the remarkable things about Jesus as a role model is His ability to infect others with His passion. When He spoke, people listened. His words carried weight because they were backed by genuine care and a deep desire to transform lives. He didn't just talk about love and compassion; He lived it out in His interactions with the marginalized, the sick, and the outcasts of society. His passion for humanity and His unwavering commitment to His purpose were infectious, drawing people from all walks of life to follow Him.

Reflecting on the impact Jesus had on His disciples and those around Him, I'm reminded of how His passion for His work was contagious. His disciples left behind their livelihoods and families to follow Him because they saw something in Him worth giving their lives to. They witnessed His miracles, heard His teachings, and experienced His love firsthand. His passion ignited a fire in their hearts that compelled them to spread His message far and wide, despite facing persecution and hardships.

In my own life, I've been fortunate to encounter teachers and mentors who share a similar passion for their work and for empowering others. Their dedication to teaching, guiding, and supporting others has left a lasting impression on me. Like Jesus, they go above and beyond to make a difference in the lives of others, inspiring me to strive for excellence and to use my own skills and talents to uplift those around me. Their passion for education and their genuine concern for the well-being of their students motivate me to pursue my goals with enthusiasm and purpose.

Jesus as a role model teaches us that passion is not just about enthusiasm; it's about a deep-seated commitment to making a positive impact in the world. His life exemplifies how passion, when coupled with love and purpose, can transform lives and bring about lasting change. As I continue on my journey, I aspire to embody His passion for justice, compassion, and serving others, knowing that His example continues to inspire countless individuals to this day.

When I think about Jesus as a role model with a clear set of values, it's like looking at a lighthouse in the midst of a stormy sea. His values were not just something He talked about; they were the guiding principles that shaped His every action and interaction. Jesus taught us that living our values means embodying them in the world, not just in words but in deeds that impact lives.

As a role model, Jesus lived His values of love, compassion, justice, and humility every day. His unwavering commitment to these principles inspired everyone around Him, from His disciples to the crowds that gathered to hear Him speak. He didn't just preach about loving one another; He demonstrated it by healing the sick, feeding the hungry, and showing kindness to the marginalized. His actions spoke louder than words and showed us what it truly means to live according to our values.

I see parallels in my own life when I think about the role models who have influenced me. They are individuals who have dedicated themselves to causes they believe in, whether it's advocating for education, fighting against poverty, or championing environmental sustainability. These role models don't just talk about their values; they actively work to make a difference in the world, showing me how to align my beliefs with meaningful action.

For instance, I've encountered spiritual leaders who go above and beyond their teaching duties to instill values of empathy and social responsibility in their members. They create opportunities for us to engage with issues like spiritual growth and humanitarian aid, helping us understand how our values can drive positive change in society. By witnessing their dedication and integrity, I've learned that living our values requires courage and perseverance, even in the face of challenges.

MY ROLE MODEL

Jesus' example teaches us that living our values isn't always easy. It requires courage to stand up for what is right, compassion to care for those in need, and humility to admit when we've made mistakes. As I strive to emulate His example, I aim to integrate my values into everything I do, knowing that each action, no matter how small, has the potential to make a difference in the lives of others. Jesus' clear set of values continues to guide and inspire me, showing me the path to becoming a role model who lives with integrity and purpose.

When I reflect on Jesus as a role model with a deep commitment to community and the world, I'm reminded of His selflessness and dedication to serving others. Jesus showed us that true greatness lies not in seeking recognition or personal gain, but in loving and caring for those around us. His life was a testament to putting others first and making a positive impact on the community.

As a role model, Jesus exemplified what it means to be other-focused rather than self-focused. He spent His days teaching, healing, and ministering to people from all walks of life. Whether it was feeding the hungry crowds, comforting the grieving, or befriending the outcasts, Jesus showed compassion and empathy in every interaction. His commitment to community was evident in His willingness to go beyond societal norms to reach those in need.

In my own life, I've been inspired by individuals who embody this same commitment to community. They are the ones who volunteer their time at local shelters, organize fundraisers for important causes, or simply lend a helping hand to a neighbor in distress. These role models show me that making a difference starts with being actively engaged in the community, whether through advocacy, service, or simply being present for those who need support.

Jesus' example challenges me to think beyond myself and consider how I can contribute to the well-being of others. It's about being aware of the needs around me and taking meaningful action to address them.

JESUS: MY ROLE MODEL

Like Jesus, I strive to be a part of my community in a way that fosters unity, compassion, and positive change. His commitment to loving others unconditionally serves as a guiding light, encouraging me to be a role model who actively seeks to make a difference in the world.

When I think about Jesus as my role model, one of the qualities that stands out most is His selflessness and acceptance of others. Jesus didn't just talk about loving your neighbour; He lived it out every day of His life. His example showed a deep compassion for people from all walks of life, regardless of their social status, background, or circumstances.

Just like Jesus, my father also exemplifies selflessness and acceptance. Growing up, I witnessed how he approached life with a genuine heart for serving others. He never allowed social barriers or differences to dictate his actions. Instead, he focused on recognizing people's needs and meeting them with compassion and practical help.

I remember countless instances where my father would roll up his sleeves and get involved, whether it was helping a neighbor fix a broken fence, volunteering at a local shelter, or simply lending a listening ear to someone going through a tough time. His lifestyle was a testament to service and acceptance, teaching me valuable lessons about the importance of caring for others and treating everyone with dignity and respect.

One particular memory that stands out is when he invited a homeless man to join us for dinner. I was initially taken aback by his gesture, but my father's kindness and willingness to see beyond the man's circumstances left a lasting impression on me. He didn't just offer a meal; he offered companionship and genuine friendship.

Through my father's example, I learned that true selflessness is about putting others' needs before your own and extending grace and acceptance to everyone, regardless of their background or past. His

MY ROLE MODEL

actions mirrored Jesus' teachings about loving your neighbour as yourself and embracing diversity with an open heart.

Today, I strive to emulate Jesus and my father by embodying selflessness and acceptance in my own life. I seek opportunities to serve others, advocate for those in need, and cultivate an inclusive environment where everyone feels valued and accepted. Jesus' example of selfless love continues to inspire me to be a role model who reflects His compassion and acceptance in everything I do.

When I reflect on Jesus as my role model, one of the most inspiring qualities He demonstrated was His ability to overcome obstacles and show that success is possible even in the face of adversity. Throughout His life and ministry, Jesus encountered numerous challenges, yet He never wavered in His mission or lost faith in His Father's plan.

One of the most profound examples of Jesus overcoming obstacles was during His earthly ministry. He faced opposition from religious leaders, skepticism from His own disciples, and misunderstanding from the crowds. Despite these challenges, Jesus remained steadfast in His commitment to proclaiming the Kingdom of God and demonstrating God's love through His words and actions.

One particular instance that stands out is when Jesus walked on water. It was a stormy night, and His disciples were struggling to row their boat across the Sea of Galilee. In the midst of the raging winds and crashing waves, Jesus appeared to them, walking effortlessly on the water. Peter, filled with both awe and doubt, asked Jesus to command him to come out onto the water too. With Jesus' assurance, Peter stepped out of the boat and began walking toward Him.

However, as Peter focused on the storm around him, fear crept in, and he started to sink. Immediately, he cried out, "Lord, save me!" Without hesitation, Jesus reached out His hand and caught Peter, saying, "You of little faith, why did you doubt?" (Matthew 14:22-33).

This miraculous moment not only displayed Jesus' supernatural power over nature but also His willingness to rescue His disciples in their moments of fear and doubt. It serves as a powerful reminder that with Jesus, we can overcome any obstacle that stands in our way.

In my own life, I have faced challenges that sometimes seemed insurmountable—academic pressures, personal struggles, and uncertainties about the future. During those times, I draw strength from Jesus' example of overcoming obstacles with unwavering faith and trust in God's plan. His life encourages me to persevere, to trust in His promises, and to believe that success is possible, no matter how daunting the circumstances may appear.

Jesus' ability to overcome obstacles serves as a beacon of hope and inspiration for me. It reminds me that with faith, courage, and determination, I can navigate life's challenges and strive toward achieving my goals. Just as Jesus demonstrated, success is not defined by the absence of obstacles but by our response to them—leaning on God's strength, trusting in His guidance, and pressing forward with hope and perseverance.

MY ROLE MODEL

MY FRIEND

Losing a friend who embodied the essence of true friendship is a wound that runs deep in my heart. It took me over 26 years to come to some form of closure to his death. Reflecting on the life of Jesus, I'm reminded of my dear friend who demonstrated such extraordinary kindness and selflessness. His name was Tihomir, whom we called Tiho, left an indelible mark on my life through his acts of love and unwavering support.

Tiho's friendship mirrored the compassion and sacrificial love that Jesus exemplified during His time on earth. Just like Jesus, Tiho went above and beyond to show his care. I remember one instance vividly when he drove seven hours from Croatia where we lived, just to surprise me with a meal from McDonald's in Italy. It wasn't just about the food; it was about the effort and thoughtfulness he put into making me feel special.

During our time together in the mission field amidst the chaos of war, Tiho's commitment to helping my wife and children stood out. Despite the dangers and challenges, he never hesitated to go out of his way to ensure our safety and well-being. His willingness to sacrifice his own comfort for the sake of others mirrored the selflessness of Jesus.

One of the most profound ways Tiho expressed his friendship was by taking me up the mountain every morning at 5 AM to pray. In those quiet moments of communion with God, Tiho taught me the importance of starting the day with spiritual grounding and seeking God's guidance. His dedication to nurturing our spiritual growth and strengthening our faith was a testament to his deep love for God and for me.

Tiho's embrace of humility and his fearless stance against racism also deeply impacted me. I recall moments when he stood up for me publicly, offering hugs and gestures of solidarity in the face of discrimination during the war with Serbia. His actions spoke volumes about his character and his unwavering commitment to standing with those who faced injustice.

Beyond these personal gestures, Tiho's friendship was marked by inclusivity and generosity. He invited me to dine in places where only the affluent usually frequented, breaking down barriers and extending hospitality to all. His example taught me that true greatness is found in humility and in serving others without reservation.

We shared many moments of spiritual significance together—praying, preaching, baptizing, and evangelizing side by side. Tiho's passion for spreading the Gospel and his eagerness to share God's love with others fueled our joint mission. His readiness to lay down his life for the sake of our friendship mirrored the sacrificial love that Jesus demonstrated for humanity.

Tragically, Tiho's life was cut short in a devastating car accident while he was on his way to meet me. The pain of losing such a faithful friend and brother in Christ is profound. Yet, his legacy of love, compassion, and unwavering friendship continues to inspire and challenge me every day. Tiho's life exemplified the essence of true friendship—the kind that mirrors the selfless love of Jesus Christ, who laid down His life for His friends. His memory remains etched in my heart as a reminder of the profound impact one life can have when lived in service to others and in devotion to God.

Choosing Tihomir as my friend was like choosing Jesus for my role model in that it was a deeply personal and enriching decision for me. One of the primary reasons I look up to Jesus is because of His unwavering friendship and compassion towards all who encountered Him, and indeed, to all who seek Him even today. Tiho embodied the qualities of Jesus that made his behaviour, example, and choices emulating in my heart.

Tiho thought me the importance of cultivating our inner spiritual life and maintaining a deep connection with God. Jesus did the same. In fact, throughout Jesus's ministry, He emphasized the significance of prayer, solitude, and communion with the Father. Jesus often withdrew to desolate places to pray, seeking divine guidance and strength for His earthly mission, and engage in self-care. His example teaches us that spiritual vitality and authenticity are essential for navigating life's challenges with grace and wisdom.

In choosing Tiho as my friend, was an example of Jesus in that I got inspired not only by what he taught me but by his entire way of life. Tiho showed me how to live authentically, love unconditionally, and serve sacrificially, just like Jesus. I was continually challenge as his friendship transform me, urging me to embody values of compassion, humility, and unwavering faith in God. His example offered guidance and inspiration every moment I spent with him, like I spend with Jesus.

Today, Tiho is not just a historical figure but a living example of what it means to be fully sold out for God and following in the footsteps of Jesus. He was a true friend, and the ultimate role model for all humanity. He humbled himself and took on the role of a servant, serving in the church and the community. A profound act of humility and a stark reminder of the importance of putting others before oneself, of serving with a genuine heart, and of embodying a spirit of selflessness in all circumstances.

Tihomir dedicated his life to sharing the good news of God's kingdom, Just like Jesus did. He taught about love, forgiveness, and reconciliation—fundamental principles that continue to resonate with relevance and power today.

I am challenged to cultivate a heart of humility, compassion, and obedience to God's will as a result of Tiho, who totally saw Jesus as his role model. His example compels me to seek opportunities to serve others, to advocate for justice and mercy, and to live out my faith in practical ways. His life continues to remind me how important it is to have a deeper understanding of what it means to follow Jesus wholeheartedly as my role model.

Choosing Jesus as my role model has been a transformative journey for me, rooted deeply in the timeless wisdom found in Philippians 2:5-8. These verses paint a vivid picture of Jesus' character—His humility, servanthood, and sacrificial love. They challenge me not just to admire Him from afar but to emulate His attitudes and actions in my own life. As I journey in faith, Jesus remains my ultimate role model—a beacon of hope, grace, and eternal truth.

GOD'S PLAN

In the of existence, God, the master Designer and Creator, envisioned a world where His beloved creations would freely commune with Him, basking in the glow of His love and offering heartfelt worship. Thus, He fashioned humanity in His perfect image, endowing them with the precious gift of choice.

Yet, as humanity made the fateful decision to turn away from God, opting instead for the path of sin, the consequences of their choice unfurled like tendrils of darkness. With each act of defiance, they unknowingly invited the shadows of suffering and affliction into their midst.

In His boundless wisdom, God, foreseeing the plight of His wayward children, orchestrated a divine plan of redemption. From the very foundation of the world, He ordained the sacrifice of His beloved Son, Jesus Christ, offering humanity a lifeline amidst the tempest of their transgressions.

Though the executor of mankind's sinful choices may be the devil, God, in His infinite mercy, does not abandon His creation to the clutches

GOD'S PLAN

of despair. Instead, He extends a beacon of hope, a pathway to salvation, even in the darkest of hours.

In His omniscience, God perceives the intricate threads of each individual's choices, from the dawn of time to the present day. He knew, with a heavy heart, the choices Adam and Eve would make, yet He also foresaw the countless souls who would turn from sin, seeking redemption and renewal.

Contrary to misconception, God is not the author of disease and suffering. Rather, He crafted a delicate framework for human existence, imbued with the freedom to choose one's path—a path that may lead to either health or affliction.

Even amidst the tumult of human frailty and sin, God's original intent remains steadfast. His desire has always been, and continues to be, the well-being and wholeness of His beloved creation. Though humanity may have stumbled into the depths of sickness and despair, God's unwavering love still shines as a beacon of hope, illuminating the path to healing and restoration.

In the concepts of existence, God's master plan unfolds with precision and purpose, weaving together the threads of creation, redemption, and restoration. To comprehend this divine blueprint, we must delve into the depths of scripture, where the wisdom of the ages is laid bare for all who seek understanding.

From the very beginning, God's master plan was set in motion—a plan born out of love and destined for eternity. In Genesis, we witness the grandeur of creation, as God spoke the universe into existence with a mere word. With each stroke of His hand, He fashioned the heavens and the earth, declaring them good. But His masterpiece was yet to come—a crown jewel to adorn His creation.

In the garden of Eden, God's master plan unfolded in earnest, as He formed man in His own image and breathed life into his lungs. Adam and Eve walked in perfect harmony with their Creator, dwelling in a paradise untouched by sin or sorrow. But alas, the serpent slithered into their midst, tempting them with the forbidden fruit and shattering the tranquility of Eden.

Yet, even in the midst of their disobedience, God's master plan remained steadfast. For in His infinite wisdom, He foresaw the fall of humanity and ordained a plan of redemption—a plan that would culminate in the sacrifice of His Son, Jesus Christ, upon the cross.

Throughout the pages of scripture, we catch glimpses of God's master plan unfolding—a tapestry woven with threads of prophecy, promise, and providence. From the covenant with Abraham to the exodus from Egypt, from the reign of kings to the cries of the prophets, every event, every moment, is part of a larger narrative—a narrative that points to the coming Messiah.

In the fullness of time, God's master plan reached its climax with the birth of Jesus Christ—a momentous occasion that would change the course of history forever. In the humble manger of Bethlehem, the Savior of the world was born, heralded by angels and adored by shepherds. And as He grew in wisdom and stature, He revealed the heart of the Father to all who would listen.

But it was upon the cross of Calvary that God's master plan was fully realized. For in the shedding of His blood, Jesus Christ atoned for the sins of humanity, offering salvation to all who would believe. Through His death and resurrection, He conquered sin and death, triumphing over the powers of darkness and securing victory for all who call upon His name.

And so, as we stand on the precipice of eternity, let us gaze upon the tapestry of God's master plan with awe and wonder. For in its intricate design, we see the fingerprints of the Creator—the Alpha and the Omega, the beginning and the end. And as we journey through the pages of scripture, may we come to understand the depths of His love and the beauty of His redemption, for truly, His master plan is a testament to His glory and grace.

MY SAVIOUR

I've always been fascinated by stories that unravel the complexities of human nature and the pursuit of knowledge. One tale that has captivated me since childhood is the age-old narrative tucked within the pages of Genesis, where the clash between temptation and obedience unfolds in the garden of Eden.

Picture this: a lush paradise teeming with vibrant life, where every leaf whispers secrets of creation and every breeze carries the scent of innocence. Here, at the heart of it all, stands the Tree of Knowledge, its fruit tantalizingly forbidden by a decree from the Divine. God's command echoes through the garden, a simple yet profound directive that sets the stage for the ultimate test of human loyalty.

In Genesis 3:1-5, we're plunged into the midst of this divine drama. It's a scene that feels strangely familiar, like a distant echo reverberating through the corridors of time. God's order is crystal clear: do not partake of the fruit from the tree of the knowledge of good and evil. It's a rule designed not to stifle but to safeguard, a boundary drawn for the protection of humanity.

Yet, as the story unfolds, we see the subtle whisperings of temptation slithering into the hearts of our first ancestors. The serpent, crafty and cunning, entices Eve with promises of enlightenment and liberation. Suddenly, the forbidden fruit seems irresistible, its allure heightened by the thrill of defiance.

In the face of temptation, Adam and Eve stand at a crossroads, torn between obedience and curiosity. It's a dilemma as old as humanity itself, a tug-of-war between the desire for knowledge and the imperative of obedience. And in that moment of decision, they choose to take matters into their own hands, forsaking God's command for the sake of self-discovery.

The narrative of the Fall reminds us of our innate vulnerability to temptation, the perennial struggle between our aspirations for wisdom and the constraints of divine decree. It speaks to our longing for autonomy and understanding, even at the cost of disobedience. Yet, woven within the fabric of this ancient tale lies a timeless truth: that our quest for knowledge must always be tempered by reverence for the wisdom of the Divine.

In the end, the story of Adam and Eve serves as a poignant reminder of our need for a saviour, a redeemer who can bridge the chasm between our aspirations and our limitations. It's a narrative that resonates across cultures and epochs, reminding us that our journey towards enlightenment is often fraught with pitfalls and perils. And yet, in the midst of our fallenness, we find hope in the promise of redemption, a promise fulfilled in the ultimate sacrifice of the One who came to save us from ourselves.

I've always been struck by the subtle yet profound shifts that occur within the human psyche when confronted with temptation. It's like watching a delicate dance between light and shadow, where every step taken brings us closer to the edge of our own frailties. Nowhere is this dance more evident than in the story of Eve's encounter with the serpent in the garden of Eden.

As I delve into Genesis 3, I find myself drawn to the pivotal moment when doubt creeps insidiously into the fertile soil of Eve's mind. The serpent, cunning and beguiling, slithers into the scene, casting doubt upon the very Word of God. It's a moment that reverberates with the echoes of every skeptic's whispered question: "Did God really say...?"

In that moment, doubt takes root, intertwining itself with the tender shoots of Eve's faith. Suddenly, the once-clear command of God becomes muddled in a haze of uncertainty. The serpent's words weave a web of confusion, tempting Eve to question the veracity of God's instructions. And like a seed planted in fertile soil, doubt begins to grow, casting its shadow over the pristine landscape of Eden.

But doubt is only the first step on a treacherous path towards disobedience. As Eve grapples with the serpent's insidious whispers, she finds herself teetering on the brink of denial. It's a subtle shift, almost imperceptible at first, as Eve begins to entertain the possibility that perhaps God's Word isn't as absolute as she once believed.

In her denial, Eve takes a dangerous leap of faith, rejecting the very foundation upon which her relationship with God is built. She chooses to trust in her own understanding rather than submitting to the authority of the Divine. It's a tragic moment, one that reverberates with the echoes of every soul who has ever chosen to walk the path of rebellion.

Yet, woven into the fabric of Eve's denial is another insidious force: pride. It's the sin that lies at the root of all disobedience, the belief that we know better than God Himself. In her pride, Eve elevates her own desires above the command of her Creator, choosing to grasp at the fleeting promise of knowledge and autonomy.

And so, in the span of a few fateful moments, Eve's journey from doubt to denial to pride mirrors the timeless struggle of humanity against the constraints of divine authority. It's a cautionary tale, reminding us of the dangers that lurk beneath the surface of our own desires. And yet, even in the midst of our rebellion, there is hope—a hope born from the promise of redemption and restoration, offered freely to all who dare to humble themselves before the Word of God.

In the journey of faith, I've come to understand that testing and trials are not just inevitable but essential. They're like the refining fires that purify gold, shaping and molding us into vessels fit for the Master's use. And in the midst of these trials, one thing becomes abundantly clear: our response to the Word of God can make all the difference.

As I reflect on Proverbs 1:1-10, I'm struck by the wisdom woven into its verses like threads in a tapestry. It's a roadmap for navigating life's tumultuous waters, a beacon of light illuminating the path of righteousness. Here, in these ancient words, lies the key to withstanding the onslaught of the enemy: acting upon the Word of God and resisting the devil.

The imagery of the tree of life resonates deeply with me, for it represents more than just a symbol of vitality and abundance—it embodies the very essence of the Word of God. Like branches stretching towards the heavens, we are called to speak forth the life-giving truth of God's Word, allowing its nourishing sap to flow through every fiber of our being.

In Proverbs 3:13,16-18, we find a profound affirmation of the life-giving power inherent in the Word of God. It's a source of wisdom and understanding, a wellspring of blessing for those who embrace its teachings. And yet, amidst the beauty of this truth, there lurks a sobering reality: the tongue has the power to wield life or death.

In Proverbs 15:4, we're confronted with the stark contrast between the wholesome tongue, which is likened to a tree of life, and the perverse tongue, which brings only brokenness and destruction. It's a reminder that our words have the power to shape our reality, to build up or tear down, to bring life or death.

But therein lies the crux of the matter: the devil seeks to tap into our tree of life, sowing seeds of doubt and discord in the fertile soil of our hearts. He whispers lies and half-truths, tempting us to believe the opposite of what God has spoken over us. And if we're not vigilant, we may find ourselves swayed by his cunning deception, yielding to fear and unbelief.

What we believe in our hearts is what we ultimately receive, for out of the abundance of the heart, the mouth speaks. The devil knows this all too well, and he capitalizes on our doubts and insecurities, seeking to uproot the truth planted within us. But if we stand firm upon the solid foundation of God's Word, if we speak forth life in the face of death, then no scheme of the enemy can prevail against us.

Reflecting on the power of Jesus' words, I'm reminded of the countless instances throughout the Gospels where His spoken word brought about instantaneous transformation. It's as if each syllable He uttered carried the weight of divine authority, shaping reality itself to conform to His will. Whatever Jesus said, whether it be healing the sick, calming the storm, or raising the dead, came to pass in the blink of an eye.

One of the most profound aspects of Jesus' ministry was His role as the sacrificial Lamb, the embodiment of innocence and purity. Despite His immense power and authority, He willingly chose to lay down His life as an atoning sacrifice for the sins of humanity. It's a testament to His boundless love and compassion, a love so deep that it was willing to endure the agony of the cross for the sake of reconciliation.

The scene in the Garden of Gethsemane serves as a poignant reminder of Jesus' divine identity and authority. In the face of imminent betrayal and arrest, He boldly declared, "I Am," invoking the sacred name of God Himself. The sheer power of His words caused the soldiers to recoil and fall to the ground, unable to withstand the overwhelming presence of the Divine.

In God's original design, His Word was intended to be the ultimate teacher, guiding humanity in the paths of righteousness and wisdom. Through His Word, He sought to impart knowledge of good and evil, riches, and honour, offering a bountiful feast for the soul. In this paradisiacal state, man would have had no need for the experience of evil, for they would have been nourished directly from the tree of life—the Word of God.

But alas, the fall of humanity shattered this idyllic vision, plunging mankind into a world marred by sin and suffering. Yet even in the midst of our brokenness, the promise of redemption echoes through the corridors of time, pointing us back to the transformative power of God's Word. It's a power that transcends human understanding, capable of bringing beauty out of ashes and life out of death.

As I contemplate the profound implications of Jesus' words and the redemptive power of God's Word, I'm reminded that even in our darkest moments, we can find hope and restoration in the promise of His unfailing love. For His Word is not just a collection of letters on a page, but a living, breathing testament to His faithfulness and grace, offering healing, restoration, and redemption to all who dare to believe.

In Genesis 5:4, there's a curious note about Adam's lifespan—it took him a staggering 900 years to learn how to die. That's a long time by anyone's standards, but the reason behind it is even more intriguing. You see, Adam had the unique privilege of feeding directly from the Word of God, which sustained him in a profound way. It was as if his connection to the divine source of life prolonged his existence far beyond what we could imagine. His physical body has to figure out how to die.

In Genesis 3:24, we encounter the imagery of the flaming sword guarding the way to the tree of life. Back in Eden, access to this life-giving tree was restricted, shrouded in mystery and guarded by divine decree. But now, through the redemptive work of Jesus Christ, that barrier has been removed. The sword, symbolizing the Word of God, points the way to eternal life, for Jesus Himself declared, "I am the way, the truth, and the life."

In Genesis 3:8, we catch a glimpse of the intimate fellowship Adam enjoyed with God in the cool of the day. It's a picture of communion and closeness, a reminder of the spiritual realm that was once accessible to humanity. The garden of Eden was more than just a physical location—it was a gateway to the spirit world, where God's presence dwelled in tangible form. And at the heart of it all stood the tree of life, a literal manifestation of Jesus Himself.

Romans 16:20 speaks of crushing Satan under our feet shortly—a declaration of victory and authority over the forces of darkness. It's a reminder that as believers, we have been given the power and authority to overcome every scheme of the enemy. Satan may roar like a lion, but he has been defeated, and it is we who stand victorious in Christ.

Deuteronomy 30:15 presents us with a choice—life or death, blessing or curse. It's a choice that lies within the realm of our free will, a decision that shapes our destiny for eternity. And when we choose life—when we embrace the Word of God with all our heart and soul—there's nothing the devil can do to thwart God's plan for our lives.

Deuteronomy 30:14 underscores the importance of aligning our heart and mouth with the Word of God. It's not enough to simply believe in our hearts; we must also confess with our mouths, declaring the truth of God's Word over our lives. Only then can we experience the fullness of God's promises and see His kingdom manifest in our midst.

In Deuteronomy 30:16, we're reminded of the blessings that come from walking in obedience to God's Word. It's not just about physical prosperity, but about experiencing abundant life in every area—spiritually, emotionally, and relationally. And wherever we go, whatever land we find ourselves in, God's favor rests upon us, blessing us beyond measure.

In Deuteronomy 30:19, we're confronted with the weight of our choices. God sets before us life and death, blessing and curse, but ultimately, the decision rests in our hands. And when we choose life—when we align our will with God's—the devil's power is rendered powerless, and we step into the fullness of God's purpose for our lives.

As I ponder 2 Chronicles 36:15, I'm struck by the relentless pursuit of God's love and mercy towards His people. Despite their stubbornness and disobedience, He never ceased sending His word, reaching out in a desperate bid to change their hearts and minds. Yet, time and time again, they turned a deaf ear to His pleas, refusing to listen and heed His warnings.

Turning back to the beginning in Genesis 3, I'm reminded of the pivotal moment when God issued a simple yet profound command to Adam and Eve: do not eat from the tree of the knowledge of good and evil. It was a directive given out of love, a boundary set for their protection and well-being. But in the cunning whispers of the serpent, doubt crept in, casting a shadow of uncertainty over God's Word.

The serpent's tactics were subtle yet effective, sowing seeds of doubt and denial in Eve's heart. First, he made her question the truth of God's command, tempting her to doubt His goodness and wisdom. Then, he outright denied the consequences of disobedience, enticing her with promises of knowledge and power. And in her desire to be like God, Eve fell into the trap of serving self rather than serving her Creator.

In Genesis 3:9, we see the tragic consequence of sin—man hiding from the presence of God in fear and shame. It's a pattern that repeats throughout history, as humanity seeks to distance itself from the One who longs to draw near. And in the aftermath of disobedience, the blame game begins, with Adam and Eve shifting responsibility onto others rather than owning up to their actions.

This pattern of blame continues to echo through the ages, manifesting in various forms of evasion and excuse-making. From blaming others to blaming God or even blaming the devil, humanity has perfected the art of shifting responsibility away from themselves. But in the end, when we stand before the judgment seat of God, there will be no one else to blame but ourselves.

Yet even in the midst of judgment, God's mercy shines through. In Genesis 3:14, we see the curse pronounced upon the serpent for allowing himself to be used by the devil. And in verse 21, we witness the first shedding of blood as God provides a better covering for Adam and Eve, foreshadowing the ultimate sacrifice of Jesus Christ on the cross.

In these ancient stories, I see reflections of my own struggles and failures, as well as the relentless pursuit of God's love and mercy towards me. And as I meditate on the lessons learned from Adam and Eve's disobedience, I'm reminded of the importance of heeding God's word, owning up to my mistakes, and embracing the forgiveness and redemption offered through Christ.

Reflecting on the character of God, I'm reminded of the profound truths that shape our understanding of His nature and attributes. One such truth is the impossibility of God lying. It's a concept that seems almost paradoxical—how can a being who is all-powerful and all-knowing be incapable of falsehood? And yet, it's precisely because of His unchanging character and integrity that God cannot lie. His word is truth, a firm foundation upon which we can anchor our lives with confidence and trust.

Another aspect of God's nature that stands out is His inability to make everyone clean. This might seem counterintuitive at first glance, especially considering His boundless power and compassion. But the reality is that while God desires all to be saved and come to the knowledge of the truth, He respects our free will and autonomy. He extends the offer of salvation to all, but ultimately, it's up to each individual to accept or reject His grace and forgiveness.

The concept of God humbling someone is another fascinating aspect of His nature. While God is certainly capable of humbling the proud and exalting the humble, true humility cannot be imposed from the outside. It must be cultivated from within, a surrender of self-will and pride to the sovereign authority of God. And yet, even in His inability to force humility upon us, God works tirelessly to draw us closer to Himself, gently nudging us towards a posture of humility and surrender.

As I contemplate these truths, I'm reminded of the profound mystery and complexity of God's nature. He is a God of love and mercy, yet He is also a God of justice and righteousness. And while there are some things He cannot do, such as lying, making everyone clean, or forcing humility upon us, His inability in these areas only serves to highlight His perfect holiness and sovereignty. In the end, it's this paradoxical nature of God that draws us ever deeper into relationship with Him, inviting us to explore the depths of His character and discover new facets of His glory with each passing day.

God's plan for revealing the woman whose seed would bruise Satan is a tapestry woven with threads of prophecy, promise, and fulfillment. It begins in the aftermath of the fall, in Genesis 3:15, where the first glimmer of hope shines through the darkness of sin and disobedience. Here, God speaks of the seed of the woman—a mysterious figure who would ultimately crush the head of the serpent, dealing a fatal blow to the forces of evil.

As the narrative unfolds, we see glimpses of this promised seed throughout the pages of Scripture. In Genesis 12:1-3, God makes a covenant with Abraham, promising that through his descendants, all nations would be blessed. This sets the stage for the emergence of a Jewish lineage through which the Messiah would ultimately come.

In 2 Samuel 7:12, God reveals to David that the promised seed would come from his own lineage, from the house of David—a line of kings and judges chosen by God to lead His people. This further narrows down the scope of the prophecy, pointing to a specific family line from which the Messiah would arise.

Isaiah 7:14 offers a startling revelation—the promised seed would be born of a virgin, a miraculous conception that defies human understanding. This prophecy serves as a signpost, marking the extraordinary nature of the Messiah's birth and the divine intervention at play in His coming.

Micah 5:2 provides a geographical clue, pinpointing the birthplace of the promised seed as Bethlehem, a small town with humble origins. Despite its insignificance in the eyes of the world, Bethlehem would serve as the cradle of the Messiah, fulfilling yet another aspect of God's intricate plan.

And in Daniel 9:25-26, we find a prophecy that not only reveals the time of the Messiah's birth but also foretells His sacrificial death. It's a sobering reminder of the dual nature of Christ's mission—to bring salvation and redemption through His birth, and to secure it through His death and resurrection.

In Matthew 2:2-5, we witness the fulfillment of these prophecies as wise men from the east journey to Bethlehem, following the star that heralds the birth of the Messiah. Their arrival in Jerusalem sparks a flurry of activity as Herod and the religious leaders scramble to understand the significance of this momentous event.

In the end, God's plan for revealing the woman whose seed would bruise Satan is a testament to His faithfulness and sovereignty. From the first promise spoken in the garden to its fulfillment in the birth of Jesus Christ, every detail has been meticulously orchestrated to bring about the redemption of humanity and the defeat of the powers of darkness.

And as we reflect on this incredible story, we're reminded of the depth of God's love and the unfathomable mystery of His ways.

Contemplating Romans 3:20, I'm struck by the stark reality it presents—that no flesh shall be justified by the deeds of the law in God's sight. It's a sobering reminder of the inadequacy of human effort to earn righteousness before a holy God. No matter how diligently we strive to keep the law, we inevitably fall short of its perfect standard. And in that realization, we come face to face with our desperate need for something—or rather, someone—greater than ourselves.

Galatians 3:21 drives this point home even further, highlighting the futility of relying on the law for salvation. If righteousness could be attained through adherence to the law, then God would have provided such a pathway for our salvation. But the truth is, no amount of rule-keeping or religious observance can bridge the gap between sinful humanity and a righteous God. We find ourselves trapped in a cycle of striving and failing, unable to break free from the chains of our own inadequacy.

And so, the need for the incarnation becomes abundantly clear. In order to fulfill the demands of the law and satisfy the requirements of divine justice, God had to come down to earth in human form. He had to take on flesh and dwell among us, experiencing firsthand the frailty and limitations of human existence. But more than that, He had to die on the cross, bearing the weight of our sin and suffering the penalty of death in our place. This He did and set the example of the perfect role Model.

THE INCARNATION

You know, there's a story that has always fascinated me, one that intertwines wonder, mystery, and a profound sense of hope. It's about the Miracle of the Incarnation, a tale that I often find myself reflecting on, especially during moments of quiet introspection.

In a world full of expectations and prophecies, something extraordinary happened. A divine presence chose to enter our world in the most humble and unexpected way—through a newborn child. As someone who often gets lost in the hustle and bustle of life, this story resonates with me because it speaks of simplicity, humility, and the awe-inspiring power of love and presence.

Picture yourself in a small, quiet town, where life is simple and people go about their daily routines, unaware that the world is about to change forever. In this unassuming setting, a young woman receives a message that she is chosen for an extraordinary purpose—to bring forth a life that embodies divinity itself. Can you imagine the mix of emotions she must have felt? The fear, the joy, the overwhelming sense of purpose?

THE INCARNATION

What strikes me most is the humility of it all. Jesus, choosing to come into the world not as a mighty king or a powerful warrior, but as a vulnerable infant. It's a reminder that sometimes, the most profound truths and the greatest miracles come to us in the simplest, most unexpected forms. This story teaches me that there is beauty in the ordinary and that miracles can occur in our everyday lives if we have the heart to see them.

The incarnation represents the ultimate act of love and sacrifice—the Creator stepping into His creation, the Eternal One entering into time, the Holy One embracing the brokenness of humanity. Through His death and resurrection, Jesus Christ became the fulfillment of prophecy, the answer to the desperate cry of humanity for redemption and reconciliation with God.

As I reflect on the profound implications of the incarnation, I'm humbled by the depth of God's love for us. In His infinite wisdom and mercy, He provided a way for us to be made righteous, not through our own efforts or merit, but through faith in the finished work of Christ on the cross. And so, I stand in awe of the miracle of the incarnation—the moment when God became flesh, dwelling among us, to bring salvation to all who believe.

I remember the first time I truly pondered the mysteries that surround the coming of the Son of God into our world. It was a quiet evening, and I found myself sitting by the window, the twilight casting a serene glow over everything. The story of the Incarnation had always been familiar to me, a tale told countless times in hushed whispers during the solemn moments of Christmas Eve. But that night, it felt different—more intimate, more real.

The idea that the divine chose to enter our earthly realm as a child, through the humble vessel of Mary, has always filled me with a sense of awe. The mystery begins with the heavenly messengers. Angels, beings of light and power, descending into our world to deliver a message that would change the course of history. I often imagine the scene: Mary, a young woman in a small, quiet town, suddenly confronted with an angelic being. What must have gone through her mind as Gabriel stood before her, proclaiming that she would bear the Son of God?

The miracle that followed was beyond human comprehension. Gabriel spoke of the Holy Spirit overshadowing Mary, and the power of the Most High coming upon her. "For that reason," he said, "the holy offspring shall be called the Son of God" (Luke 1:35). It was a divine promise, a moment where heaven touched earth in a way that defied all natural laws.

As I reflected on this, I couldn't help but think of how often we encounter situations that seem insurmountable, where the odds are stacked against us. Mary must have felt a whirlwind of emotions—fear, uncertainty, awe. Yet, she responded with faith, embracing the mystery and the miracle with a heart open to the impossible.

Gabriel's reassurance to Mary has always struck a chord with me: *"For nothing will be impossible with God"* (Luke 1:37). It's a statement that echoes through the ages, a reminder that when God is involved, the ordinary transforms into the extraordinary. I find myself holding onto these words during times of doubt and difficulty, when the path ahead seems unclear. They are a beacon of hope, a reminder that the divine can work in mysterious ways, far beyond our understanding.

The miracle of the Incarnation teaches me that God's plans often unfold in ways that defy human logic. Mary's story is a testament to the fact that the divine can break into our lives in the most unexpected of ways, bringing with it a promise of new life and hope. It challenges me to look beyond the surface, to seek the deeper meaning in the events of my life, and to trust that even in the midst of confusion and uncertainty, there is a purpose being woven by hands far greater than mine.

THE INCARNATION

As I sit by the window, lost in these thoughts, I am reminded of the countless miracles that happen around us every day—miracles that, like the Incarnation, often go unnoticed or are misunderstood. The birth of a child, the healing of a broken heart, the beauty of a sunset—these are all reflections of the divine, moments where heaven touches earth and the impossible becomes possible.

The story of the Incarnation is not just an ancient tale; it is a living reality, a reminder that God is with us, working in and through us in ways that we may not always understand. It calls me to embrace the mystery, to welcome the miracles, and to live with a heart full of wonder and gratitude for the extraordinary gift of the divine presence in our everyday lives.

As I close my eyes, I can almost hear the angel's voice, gentle yet powerful, whispering in the depths of my soul, *"For nothing will be impossible with God."* And in that moment, I find peace, knowing that the same power that brought forth the Son of God into our world is at work in my life, guiding me, loving me, and transforming the ordinary into the miraculous.

There are moments in life that challenge us to look beyond the ordinary, to believe in something greater than ourselves. For me, one of those moments was when I first truly contemplated the miraculous conception of Jesus Christ. The story of a young woman, Mary, chosen to bring forth a child without a human father, defied everything I knew about the world. It was a narrative that not only sparked wonder but also fulfilled a deep, intrinsic longing for something eternal.

Growing up, I often heard the Christmas story—the angels, the shepherds, the birth in a humble manger. It was a beautiful tale, but it wasn't until I delved into the heart of the story that I began to grasp its profound significance. Imagine, for a moment, a world awaiting salvation, a people yearning for a light in their darkest hour. And then, out of the blue, comes a message of hope: a saviour would be born, not in grandeur or splendor, but through a simple, humble virgin.

The miraculous element of Christ's birth lies in its very nature—Jesus was conceived in Mary by the Holy Spirit, without a human father. This wasn't just a story to make headlines; it was a divine intervention, a supernatural event that transcended the laws of nature. Jesus, the Messiah, Immanuel—God with us—would have a birth unlike any other. He was not just another human teacher or a moral guide. He was God incarnate, stepping into our world to offer a salvation that no human savior could provide.

A saviour born of natural means could never fulfill the divine purpose needed to rescue humanity from its deepest flaws and gravest emergencies. I often think about the crises we face in our lives—the moments when all seems lost, when human help falls short. In those times, I crave something beyond today, something that touches eternity. A savior tainted by sin would be powerless to save me from my own shortcomings and the brokenness of this world. We needed, I needed, a saviour who was both fully divine and fully human—someone who could bridge the gap between heaven and earth.

God's solution to our deepest needs came in the form of the virgin birth, a miraculous event that ensured Jesus would have a sinless nature. This wasn't just about fulfilling a prophecy; it was about meeting humanity's need for a perfect savior. Jesus, the God-man, embodies both the divine and the human, making Him the perfect mediator between us and God. He alone could offer the salvation that our hearts desperately seek because He alone is God.

I remember reading the account of the shepherds in the Gospel of Luke. Picture this: shepherds, watching over their flocks in the stillness of the night, when suddenly the sky bursts open with the light and glory of heavenly beings. An angel appears, bringing a message that would echo through the ages:

THE INCARNATION

"Do not be afraid; for behold, I bring you good news of great joy which will be for all the people; for today in the city of David there has been born for you a Savior, who is Christ the Lord" (Luke 2:10-11).

As if the angel's message wasn't astonishing enough, the whole sky filled with a multitude of heavenly hosts, praising God and proclaiming peace on earth. It's hard to imagine the awe and fear the shepherds must have felt, standing under that starlit sky, witnessing the divine proclamation of a saviour's birth. I try to put myself in their place, feeling the chill of the night air, the roughness of the ground beneath my feet, and then being engulfed in a brilliant, celestial light that speaks of hope and redemption.

When I think about that tiny baby, lying in a manger, I realize that He is the same one John speaks of when he says, *"In the beginning was the Word, and the Word was with God, and the Word was God. He was in the beginning with God"* (John 1:1-2). It's mind-blowing to consider that this baby, vulnerable and small, is the very embodiment of God—the same divine Word that spoke the universe into existence.

It all becomes clear when I replace *"Word"* with *"Christ"* in John's gospel:

"In the beginning was the Christ, and the Christ was with God, and the Christ was God. He was in the beginning with God. All things came into being through Christ; and apart from Him nothing came into being that has come into being. In Christ was life; and the life was the light of men" (John 1:1-4).

Christ, who was with God from the beginning, chose to enter our world, to bring life and light into our darkness. This realization fills me with a profound sense of gratitude and hope. It's a reminder that no matter how bleak things may seem, the light of Christ shines bright, offering salvation and eternal life to all who believe.

JESUS: MY ROLE MODEL

Reflecting on the miraculous conception and birth of Jesus fills me with a sense of wonder and a renewed faith in the divine plan. It reminds me that in a world filled with uncertainty and turmoil, there is a constant source of hope and salvation in the person of Jesus Christ, the God-man who came to save us all.

It was one of those evenings when the world seemed to slow down, and I found myself sitting quietly, reflecting on the complexities of life. My thoughts wandered to the concept of a mediator, someone who stands in the gap between two opposing sides, bringing them together. It struck me how vital this role is, not just in legal or personal disputes, but in the grander scheme of things, especially in our relationship with the divine.

Growing up, I often felt the disconnect between the world as it is and the world as it should be. There was a sense of longing, a feeling that something was missing. It wasn't just about the daily struggles or the inevitable ups and downs of life. It was deeper, a yearning for a connection that went beyond the physical and touched the spiritual. I realized that to bridge this gap, we needed someone who could fully understand both sides—someone who was both divine and human.

The idea that a mediator had to be both God and man made perfect sense to me, especially as I pondered the role of Jesus Christ. On one hand, we needed someone who could relate to our human experiences, who understood our struggles, our joys, and our pains. On the other hand, this mediator also needed to have the divine authority to bring about true reconciliation and salvation.

I think back to moments when I felt overwhelmed by life's challenges, when no amount of human wisdom or support seemed enough. During those times, I found solace in the thought of a mediator who not only understood my plight but also had the power to transform my situation. This mediator had to be God, for only God could offer the grace and strength needed to overcome the deepest of life's hurdles.

THE INCARNATION

At the same time, the mediator had to be human to truly grasp our condition. It's one thing to sympathize from a distance, but it's another to empathize through shared experience. Jesus, the God-man, fits this role perfectly. He walked among us, felt hunger, pain, joy, and sorrow. He lived the human experience in its entirety, yet without the flaw of sin. This unique combination of divinity and humanity makes Him the perfect bridge between us and God. It makes Him the perfect role model.

I remember reading about the high priests of the Old Testament, who acted as mediators between God and the people. They offered sacrifices and prayed on behalf of the people, but even they were limited by their own human nature. They couldn't fully embody both the divine and the human. The more I thought about it, the more I realized the profound need for a mediator who transcends these limitations, someone who could truly unite heaven and earth.

This need for a divine-human mediator is beautifully encapsulated in the life of Jesus. He wasn't just a messenger from God or a holy man with extraordinary insight. He was God in the flesh, living among us, bridging the gap that had separated humanity from its Creator. His birth, life, death, and resurrection are all testament to this unique role. As I reflected on this, I felt a deep sense of gratitude and awe for the lengths to which God went to reconcile us to Himself.

One of the most striking moments in the Gospels is when Jesus stands before the people, fully embodying both natures. As He healed the sick, comforted the broken-hearted, and forgave sins, He demonstrated His divine authority and deep compassion. In these acts, I see a glimpse of what true mediation looks like—understanding the depth of human need and responding with divine love and power.

I often think about the night in the Garden of Gethsemane, where Jesus prayed in deep anguish, knowing the suffering that lay ahead. In that moment, He fully embraced His humanity, experiencing fear and sorrow, yet He also submitted to His divine mission to save humanity.

His willingness to bear the weight of our sins and bridge the gap between us and God is the ultimate act of mediation.

When I face my own moments of fear and uncertainty, I draw strength from Jesus' example. Knowing that He has walked this path before me and has the power to guide me through my own struggles gives me hope and courage. He is the mediator who not only understands my human condition but also offers divine assistance and grace.

As I sat there that evening, reflecting on these truths, I felt a renewed sense of peace. The realization that we have a mediator who is both God and man brought a clarity to my understanding of salvation and reconciliation. Jesus, in His unique role, provides the perfect solution to the deepest needs of my heart and soul. He bridges the gap between heaven and earth, offering me a way to connect with the divine and find true peace and purpose.

In the quiet of that evening, I felt a deep gratitude for this divine mediator who loves us so much that He chose to step into our world, to walk among us, and to bring us back into a relationship with God. This realization fills me with a sense of wonder and a renewed commitment to follow Him, knowing that in Jesus, I have found the perfect bridge between heaven and earth.

THE INCARNATION

GOD *clothed* HIMSELF

I remember the first time the idea of God becoming human truly struck me. I was sitting in the back pew of a small church, the kind with creaky wooden floors and stained glass windows that cast colourful patterns on the walls at Upper room Pentecostal Church, Williamsville. It was a chilly evening about 28 degrees Celsius, and the warmth inside the church was comforting, almost like a gentle embrace. As the pastor began to speak about the Incarnation, I found myself captivated by the notion that the infinite Creator of the universe could take on human form and walk among us.

The thought of God clothing Himself in flesh seemed both miraculous and bewildering. How could the divine, so vast and boundless, fit into the fragile frame of a human being? It was like trying to imagine the ocean contained within a single drop of water. Yet, the more I pondered it, the more it made sense in the context of love—a love so profound that it sought to bridge the gap between heaven and earth.

Growing up, I'd always heard about Jesus being born in a manger, surrounded by animals and humble shepherds. It was a nice story, one that brought warmth and joy during the Christmas season. But it wasn't until I considered the depth of what that night in Bethlehem represented that I began to appreciate its full significance. It was more than just the birth of a child; it was God choosing to become one of us, to experience our struggles, our joys, and our pains firsthand.

I often wondered why God would choose to enter the world in such a humble way, as a baby born to a young, unassuming couple in a small town. It seemed so contrary to what I would expect from a divine entrance. If I were God, I might have opted for a grand display of power and glory, something that would leave no doubt about my identity. But that's the beauty of it, I realized—God's ways are not our ways. By coming to us as a vulnerable infant, God showed a different kind of strength, one rooted in humility and love.

The mystery of the Incarnation became even more poignant for me as I faced my own challenges and uncertainties in life. There were times when I felt overwhelmed, when the weight of the world seemed too heavy to bear. During those moments, the idea of a God who understands my struggles because He has lived through them brought immense comfort. Knowing that Jesus walked the same dusty roads, felt the same weariness, and experienced the same sorrows as I do, made Him feel close and relatable, not distant or unreachable.

One particular evening, as I was struggling with a difficult decision, I found myself turning to the story of the Incarnation for guidance. It dawned on me that God's choice to become flesh was an act of solidarity with humanity, a way of saying, *"I am with you, no matter what."* This realization gave me a new perspective on my own life's struggles and reminded me that I am never truly alone.

As I sat there in that little church, listening to the pastor's words, I felt a deep connection to the divine story of God becoming human. It wasn't just an abstract theological concept anymore; it was a living reality that touched my heart and soul. The Incarnation showed me that

God's love is not just a distant, abstract force, but a tangible presence that meets us in our everyday lives, in our joys and our sorrows.

Reflecting on how God clothed Himself in flesh has forever changed the way I view my relationship with the divine. It's a reminder that God is not some far-off deity, but a loving presence that understands our humanity in the most intimate way. It's a story that continues to inspire me, filling me with awe and gratitude for the incredible love that would lead the Creator of the universe to become one of us.

So, whenever I feel the weight of the world pressing down on me, I think back to that small church and the warmth of that evening, and I remember the profound truth that God chose to walk this earth as one of us. It's a truth that brings light into the darkest moments and hope into the most difficult trials, reminding me that God's love is always near, wrapped in the very flesh of humanity.

I've always been fascinated by the complexities of the human experience—the way we're able to feel such a range of emotions, make decisions, and experience the world through our senses. But it wasn't until I delved into the deeper spiritual aspects of our existence that I began to truly appreciate how we are more than just flesh and blood. One passage that resonates deeply with me is John 4:24, where it says, *"God is Spirit, and those who worship Him must worship in spirit and truth."*

This verse led me on a journey of understanding the essence of who we are and how we relate to the divine. The concept of the Incarnation, where God took on human flesh, became a pivotal part of this exploration. The term "Incarnation" comes from the Latin word meaning *"in flesh."* It's the idea that the infinite, all-powerful God chose to manifest Himself in a human body, to be clothed in the very same flesh that we inhabit.

GOD CLOTHED HIMSELF

One evening, while sitting with a group of friends, we discussed what it means to be truly spiritual in a world that often emphasizes the physical and material. It struck me that many of us, myself included, sometimes fall into the trap of being "carnal Christians," or as one of my friends humorously put it, "meatheads." We get so caught up in the tangible, day-to-day aspects of life that we forget about our spiritual nature.

"May your whole spirit, soul and body be kept blameless at the coming of our Lord Jesus Christ." 1 Thessalonians 5:23

This verse was a revelation to me. It reminded me that we are not just physical beings; we are spirit, we have a soul, and we live in a body. It's a profound truth that aligns with the essence of God, who is Spirit. We, too, are spiritual beings at our core, designed to connect with the divine in a way that transcends our physical form.

Reflecting on the Incarnation, I realized that when God became flesh, He didn't violate any laws of nature. Instead, He worked within the very framework He created. He placed His Spirit within a woman, allowing Himself to take on flesh and enter our world. It's a beautiful reminder of how the spiritual and physical are intricately intertwined. Just as we, in the act of creation, contribute the physical body, God breathes life into that body by imparting a spirit.

"Remember Him—before the silver cord is severed, and the golden bowl is broken; before the pitcher is shattered at the spring, and the wheel broken at the well, and the dust returns to the ground it came from, and the spirit returns to God who gave it." Ecclesiastes 12:6-7

This passage made me reflect on the cycle of life and death, where our physical bodies return to the earth, but our spirits return to God. It's a cycle that highlights our dual nature as both physical and spiritual beings.

Zechariah 12:1 adds another layer to this understanding: *"The Lord, who stretches out the heavens, who lays the foundation of the earth, and who forms the human spirit within a person."* It's awe-inspiring to think that each of us has a spirit formed by God, a unique essence that makes us who we are. This realization brought a new sense of purpose and significance to my life, knowing that I am more than just a collection of cells and atoms.

One of the most touching moments for me was reading Psalm 139:13-16, which speaks of how God knitted us together in our mother's womb and knew us before we were born. It's a passage that underscores the intimate connection between the Creator and His creation. It reminded me that my life is not just a random occurrence but part of a divine plan, carefully and lovingly crafted by God.

Hebrews 12:9 refers to God as the *"Father of spirits,"* which brought everything full circle for me. It reinforced the idea that our true identity lies not in our physical bodies but in our spiritual essence. As I navigated through life's challenges, this understanding gave me a deeper sense of peace and confidence, knowing that my spirit is connected to God, the source of all life.

One particular experience stands out in my memory, illustrating the significance of our spiritual nature. A close friend of mine had just welcomed a new baby into the world, and as I held that tiny, delicate life in my arms, I was overwhelmed by the miracle of creation. It was a poignant reminder of how we, as human beings, contribute the physical form, while God breathes life into that form, placing a spirit within. Although Kathleen and I had seven babies and they are now all adults, that moment of seeing a new life always remind me of the miracle of creation.

In that moment, I felt a profound connection to the divine mystery of life, a reminder that we are more than our bodies, more than our earthly existence. We are spiritual beings, created by a loving God who chose to walk among us in the flesh, to experience our world firsthand and to offer us a way to connect with Him on a deeper, spiritual level.

Reflecting on all of this, I've come to realize that our journey on earth is not just about navigating the physical world but about embracing our spiritual nature and deepening our relationship with God. The Incarnation, God clothing Himself in flesh, is a powerful testament to this truth. It's a reminder that no matter what challenges we face or how lost we may feel, our spirits are eternally connected to the divine, guiding us toward a deeper understanding of who we are and our place in God's creation.

It was a brisk autumn evening, and I was curled up in my favorite armchair, sipping on a warm cup of tea, when the topic of spirits suddenly came to mind. It's one of those subjects that had always fascinated me but also left me with more questions than answers. What exactly are spirits, and how do they interact with our lives? The more I thought about it, the more I realized that the world of spirits is vast and varied, encompassing everything from angelic beings to the very essence of God's presence.

As a child, I was captivated by stories of angels and demons. I imagined angels as magnificent beings with shining wings and radiant faces, messengers of God who appeared in moments of great significance. And demons dark and ugly trying to scare people.

My grandmother often spoke of her belief in guardian angels, divine protectors assigned to watch over us. She'd recount how she felt an unseen hand guiding her through difficult times, and it comforted me to think that I too had an angel looking out for me.

Over time, my understanding of angelic spirits deepened. Angels, I learned, are not just protectors but also servants of God, carrying out His will and delivering His messages. In the Bible, there are countless instances of angels appearing to humans, offering guidance and strength. One story that particularly resonated with me was when an angel appeared to Mary, announcing the miraculous birth of Jesus. It's incredible to think that these spiritual beings can bridge the gap between heaven and earth, bringing us closer to the divine.

Then there are human spirits, the essence of who we are. I came to understand that each of us possesses a unique spirit, a spark of life breathed into us by God. This realization was both humbling and empowering. It meant that we are more than just our physical bodies; we are spiritual beings on a journey. I recall a moment of clarity one evening as I stood on a hill where we lived up at Rebecca Richmond Road, Guaracara, looking out over the vast landscape. The wind gently rustled the leaves, and I felt a profound connection to something greater than myself. It was as if my spirit was awakening to the divine presence within and around me.

Human spirits, I believe, carry the imprint of God's image. They reflect our deepest desires, our capacity for love, and our quest for meaning. Each person's spirit is a unique blend of strengths and weaknesses, hopes and fears, all woven together in a tapestry that tells the story of who we are. Understanding this has helped me appreciate the individuality of each person I encounter, recognizing that we are all on our own spiritual journeys.

Of course, the Holy Spirit is a concept that has always fascinated and comforted me. I think of the Holy Spirit as God's presence within us, a guide, a counsellor, and a source of strength. One of the most transformative moments in my spiritual journey was when I felt the gentle nudge of the Holy Spirit prompting me to take a leap of faith. I was at a crossroads in my life, unsure of which path to take, when I felt a deep sense of peace and clarity. It was as if an unseen force was guiding me, and I knew in my heart that it was the Holy Spirit leading me toward my true purpose.

The Holy Spirit is often described as a comforting presence, like a gentle breeze that whispers words of encouragement and hope. I've experienced this comfort in times of grief and uncertainty, feeling an inexplicable sense of peace wash over me, assuring me that I am not alone. The Holy Spirit's role as a guide has also been crucial in my decision-making, helping me discern the right path and giving me the courage to follow it.

On the flip side, there's also the reality of demonic spirits, which can be unsettling to think about. I've always been a bit skeptical about the idea of evil spirits, chalking it up to superstitions or the stuff of horror movies. But as I delved deeper into my faith, I began to realize that the existence of demonic spirits is acknowledged in many religious traditions, including Christianity. These spirits are often seen as forces that seek to disrupt, deceive, and destroy.

I remember a particularly dark period in my life when I felt a constant cloud of negativity hanging over me. No matter what I did, I couldn't shake the feeling of being weighed down by something unseen. It was during this time that a wise friend suggested that I pray for protection against negative spiritual influences. Skeptical but desperate, I followed her advice, and to my surprise, I began to feel a sense of relief and freedom. It was as if a heavy burden had been lifted from my shoulders, and I realized that there are indeed forces at work that we cannot see but can certainly feel.

Understanding the existence of demonic spirits has made me more vigilant and mindful of the spiritual battles we face. It's a reminder that we must guard our hearts and minds, staying connected to the divine and relying on the strength of the Holy Spirit to overcome these negative influences. It's not about living in fear but rather about being aware and equipped to stand strong in our faith.

Reflecting on the different types of spirits—angelic, human, Holy, and demonic—has given me a richer understanding of the spiritual dimensions of our lives. It's a complex and often mysterious realm, but one that is deeply intertwined with our everyday experiences. Whether it's the comforting presence of the Holy Spirit, the protection of angelic beings, or the challenges posed by demonic forces, these spirits shape our journey and help us navigate the path we walk.

As I continue on my spiritual journey, I am grateful for the insights I've gained and the experiences that have deepened my understanding of the world of spirits. Each encounter and every revelation has brought me closer to the divine, reminding me that we are all part of a larger, interconnected spiritual reality. It's a journey that is both humbling and inspiring, and one that I am committed to exploring with an open heart and a spirit attuned to the divine.

I vividly recall a time when I sat at the kitchen table, my Bible open, contemplating the mysteries of life and faith. I was drawn to Romans 7:8-9, where Paul speaks about the age of accountability—a concept that had always intrigued me. According to Paul, sin becomes an active force in our lives when we reach an age where we can distinguish right from wrong. Before that, we are like innocent children, spiritually alive and unburdened by sin.

This idea of an age of accountability got me thinking about how we start our journey in this world. When a child is born, they are pure, untouched by the complexities and corruption that come with age. It's a beautiful thought, one that paints a picture of innocence and hope. However, as we grow, we inevitably encounter the realities of sin and moral choices, marking the transition from innocence to accountability.

As I delved deeper into this concept, my thoughts turned to Jesus, who was not only born of a woman but was also God clothed in flesh. This is a profound mystery, one that intertwines the divine with the human in a way that defies simple explanation. Jesus was God's spirit, incarnate—God placing His spirit in a woman, and she, in turn, clothing

GOD CLOTHED HIMSELF

Him in flesh. It's a concept that resonates deeply with me, illustrating how the divine and the human can coexist in a single person.

The story of Jesus' birth is one I've heard countless times, yet it never loses its wonder. Luke 1:26-35 describes the moment when the angel Gabriel appeared to Mary, telling her that she would conceive a son by the power of the Holy Spirit. God put His spirit into the virgin Mary, and she clothed Him with flesh. Jesus wasn't just the Son of God; He was God in the flesh, born of an incorruptible seed. This realization is both awe-inspiring and humbling, reminding me of the immense love and sacrifice involved in the Incarnation.

Mary's reaction to the angel's message, as described in verse 29, always struck a chord with me. She was troubled, as any of us would be if confronted with such a profound revelation. It made me think about how we should approach the unknown and the divine with a sense of humility and openness. It's a reminder to be swift to hear and slow to speak, especially when faced with things beyond our everyday experience. We don't have visions every day, no matter how spiritual we think we are, and when we do, they can be both daunting and transformative.

Jeremiah 31:22 talks about a new thing God would do—a woman encompassing a man. This prophecy points to Mary and the virgin birth, where she, a woman, would bear God's son. The word "compass" in this context means to surround or be around, signifying Mary's role in bringing the divine into the world through her flesh. It's a beautiful imagery of how the divine is surrounded and brought into being through human participation.

The notion of God clothing Himself in flesh is further illuminated in John 1:1, 14, where it says, *"The Word was made flesh and dwelt among us, and we beheld His glory."* This verse encapsulates the heart of the Incarnation—God's word becoming flesh and living among us. The term "dwelt" here means to pitch a tent or encamp. It's a striking image,

JESUS: MY ROLE MODEL

suggesting that God, in taking on flesh, set up camp among us, choosing to live within our world and experience life as we do.

I often reflect on the idea of *"pitching a tent"* as a metaphor for our earthly existence. Just as God temporarily pitched His tent among us in the form of Jesus, our lives here on earth are also temporary. When we die, it's as if we are folding our tent and moving on to a new address, a new dimension. This perspective helps me to see life as a journey, with each of us carrying our tents, ready to move on to our next destination when the time comes.

One winter evening, as I walked through a quiet forest blanketed in snow, I felt a deep connection to these ideas. The trees stood tall and still, like silent witnesses to the divine presence that had once walked the earth. I imagined Jesus, God in flesh, walking among us, experiencing the same cold and beauty that I felt. It made the concept of the Incarnation incredibly real and tangible, a reminder that God is not distant but intimately involved in the world.

Understanding that God clothed Himself in flesh helps me see the divine in the mundane aspects of life. Every interaction, every challenge, and every moment is an opportunity to encounter the sacred. It reminds me that we are all part of a larger story, one that began with a virgin giving birth to a child who was both fully human and fully divine.

As I continue to explore and reflect on these mysteries, I am filled with a sense of wonder and gratitude. The Incarnation is not just a theological concept but a profound reality that shapes how I view my life and my relationship with God. It's a story that reminds me of the incredible love and sacrifice that God has for each of us, choosing to walk among us and experience our world firsthand.

This understanding has profoundly impacted my spiritual journey, helping me to see the divine in every aspect of my life and to approach each day with a sense of purpose and reverence. Whether in the quiet moments of reflection or the busy rush of daily life, I am constantly reminded that God is with us, clothed in flesh, walking beside us on this journey.

I remember it vividly, the first time I truly grasped the profound idea of God pitching His tent among us. It was a quiet evening, and I was sitting outside, gazing at the stars. The air was crisp, and the world seemed to pause for a moment, allowing me to ponder the depths of John's Gospel. *"In the beginning was the Word, and the Word was with God, and the Word was God....All things came to be through him, and without him nothing came to be....And the Word became flesh...."* These words, so rich and evocative, captured my imagination like never before.

John's prologue presents this grand vision where all creation emerges from the Word, God's own self-expression, who chose to become flesh in the person of Jesus. It's a narrative that has always fascinated me, not just because of its theological depth but because it speaks to a profound truth about God's relationship with humanity. The idea that the Creator of the universe would take on human form and live among us is nothing short of awe-inspiring.

As I reflected on this, I thought about the significance of the Incarnation. For John, this act of God becoming flesh was the ultimate expression of divine love, a supreme act that brought about salvation not through sacrifice or atonement, but through intimacy, friendship, and mutuality. It's a perspective that resonates deeply with me. Often, we get so caught up in the sacrificial imagery of Jesus' death that we overlook the profound implications of His life and presence among us.

One evening, I found myself lost in thought about how John's Gospel differs from the other Gospels. While Mark, for instance, speaks of Jesus' death as a ransom, John's narrative doesn't dwell on themes of sacrifice or atonement. Instead, it emphasizes the relationship between God and humanity, highlighting the desire for a close, personal connection with each of us. This shift in focus opened my eyes to a new understanding of what it means to be saved.

Thinking back, I remember a particular Sunday service that brought this to life for me. Our pastor spoke about how we often merge the different Gospel accounts into one narrative, missing the unique perspectives each one offers. John's Gospel, with its focus on the Incarnation and the revelation of God's love through Jesus, presents a portrait of Jesus that emphasizes His role as a friend and guide, rather than a sacrificial lamb. This perspective challenges us to see God not as a distant deity demanding sacrifice but as a loving presence wanting to share divine life with us.

As I mulled over these ideas, I found myself drawn to the image of God pitching His tent among us. It's such a humble, approachable metaphor. I pictured Jesus walking among us, experiencing our joys and sorrows, and sharing in the very fabric of human life. This wasn't just a temporary visit but a deliberate choice to dwell with us, to be intimately involved in our lives. It's a reminder that God's presence is not confined to the heavens but is woven into the very fabric of our existence.

One summer, as I went camping with our seven children and their spouses, the reality of this image struck me even more. We had set up our tents and gathered around a campfire, the warmth and light cutting through the darkness. It dawned on me that this is what God's presence in the world is like—a source of warmth and light in the midst of our often cold and dark realities. The Word became flesh and set up His tent among us, bringing light and life to a weary world.

This understanding transformed my faith. It made me realize that the essence of the Incarnation is about God sharing life with us in a tangible, personal way. It's about the divine reaching down to lift us up, not through grand gestures of sacrifice but through simple acts of love and presence. Jesus' life, death, and resurrection are a testament to this profound truth, a declaration that God's deepest desire is to share divine life with us.

Reflecting on John 3:16, I was struck by how it encapsulates this idea: *"For God so loved the world that He gave His only Son, so that everyone who believes in Him may not perish but may have eternal life."* This verse, often quoted, is a powerful reminder of the lengths to which God went to demonstrate His love. It's not about appeasing an angry deity but about a loving Father extending an invitation to eternal life.

One evening, while reading through John's "Farewell Address" (John 13:1–17:26), I was moved by the themes of friendship and service that permeate Jesus' words. He speaks of love, not as a command, but as a natural outflow of a life lived in close relationship with God. Jesus' call to love one another as He has loved us is a powerful mandate that underscores the importance of mutuality and faithful love in our lives. It's a call to be a reflection of the divine love that has been so generously extended to us.

Understanding that God's ultimate goal is our full flourishing reshaped my view of salvation. It's not just about being saved from something but being saved for something—a life of purpose, intimacy, and love. It's about experiencing the fullness of life that comes from living in close relationship with the divine, a life where we are constantly growing, evolving, and becoming more like the God who pitched His tent among us.

As I continue to walk this journey of faith, I am continually amazed by the depth of God's love and the lengths to which He has gone to be with us. The Incarnation is not just a historical event but a present reality that shapes how I see the world and my place in it. It's a story of divine love and human response, a story that continues to unfold in my life and in the lives of those around me. And for that, I am deeply grateful.

I remember the first time I sat down with the letters to the Colossians and the Ephesians, feeling a sense of awe and wonder. These texts, written in the tradition of Paul, offer a grand, cosmic vision that stretches from the dawn of creation to the final fulfillment of God's plan. They reveal a remarkable belief that Christ is the image of the invisible God, a concept that struck me deeply as I pondered its implications.

One evening, as I was sitting in my cozy living room, the letters took on a new life. The fire crackled softly, and the room was bathed in the warm glow of the flickering flames. I read through Colossians and Ephesians, captivated by the idea that God chose believers before the foundation of the world. It was a humbling thought, realizing that before time even began, God had a plan, a vision that included each one of us.

Colossians speaks of Christ as the image of the invisible God, a notion that seemed almost too grand to comprehend. I imagined a vast tapestry, woven with threads of divine intention, stretching from eternity past to eternity future. Each thread represented a part of God's plan, with Christ at the very center, holding everything together. It's a vision that reminds me of the intricate patterns we see in nature, where every detail, no matter how small, is part of a larger, harmonious whole.

Ephesians builds on this by stating that the goal of God's plan was the coming of Christ. It's a declaration that everything, from the smallest atom to the vastness of the cosmos, finds its origin and purpose in Christ. I found myself marveling at the idea that not only did everything begin with Christ, but it is also sustained and will ultimately be fulfilled in God through Him. It's a belief that infuses every aspect of life with meaning and purpose, a reminder that we are part of a grand, divine narrative.

One particular passage that caught my attention was Philippians 2:7-11. Jesus chose to live as a man, operating within the limitations of humanity. This decision was profound because it meant that we, too, could follow in His footsteps and perform the works He did, as He promised in John 14:12. It's a promise that fills me with hope and a sense of responsibility, knowing that we are called to carry on the work of Christ in the world.

I recall a conversation with a friend who struggled to understand why Jesus, who was God in the flesh, would choose to strip Himself of His divine attributes. We sat in a quiet café, sipping our coffee, as I explained that Jesus wanted to show us what it means to live fully human, dependent on God's Spirit. By doing so, He demonstrated that the same Spirit that empowered Him is available to us, enabling us to live out God's plan in our own lives.

Jesus' ministry, was unique in the sense that He operated solely as a human being and God in the flesh, filled and guided by the Holy Spirit. It meant that the miracles and acts of love and compassion that Jesus performed were not out of reach for us. We, too, can participate in God's work, empowered by the same Spirit that moved through Jesus. It's a truth that has motivated me to step out in faith, knowing that God can work through my ordinary life to accomplish extraordinary things.

I remember another moment of reflection, standing by the shore of a vast, calm lake in Toronto, lake Ontario, the water reflecting the sky like a mirror. It was there that I truly grasped the significance of Jesus' choice to live as a man. In the quiet of that serene setting, I understood that by becoming fully human, Jesus showed us the way to live in communion with God. His life was a blueprint for us to follow, a demonstration of how to live in alignment with God's will.

One aspect that continues to fascinate me is the idea that Jesus, even in His glorified body, still bears the scars of His crucifixion. It's a poignant reminder that His humanity and sacrifice are eternally significant. These scars are not marks of defeat but of victory, a testament to His love and commitment to us. They remind me that God's plan is not just about the grand cosmic vision but also about the intimate, personal journey each of us is on.

JESUS: MY ROLE MODEL

As I read through the "Farewell Address" in John's Gospel (John 13:1-17:26), I was struck by the themes of friendship, service, and faithful love. Jesus spoke about His deep love for His disciples, a love that extends to each one of us. It's a love that is rooted in the desire for our full flourishing, for us to live lives that reflect God's glory. This address is a powerful testament to God's ultimate plan for humanity—a plan that invites us into a relationship of intimacy and mutuality with the divine.

Reflecting on all of this, I am filled with a sense of awe and gratitude for the way God's plan has unfolded throughout history and continues to unfold in my life. It's a plan that encompasses not just the grand, cosmic scale but also the everyday details of my journey. Knowing that I am part of this divine narrative gives me a sense of purpose and direction, motivating me to live in a way that reflects the love and grace of the God who pitched His tent among us.

As I continue to walk this path, I am constantly reminded of the profound truth that Christ, the image of the invisible God, holds all things together. This knowledge fills me with hope and a deep sense of responsibility to live out my faith in a way that honors God's plan for the fullness of time. It's a journey that I am honored to be a part of, and one that I look forward to continuing with each step I take.

I've always been intrigued by the life of Jesus, not just as a historical figure, but as someone whose existence shaped the course of humanity. When I read Acts 10:38, it hit me differently than before. It says Jesus was anointed by the Holy Spirit to do the works. Anointed? I thought, wasn't Jesus God Himself? Shouldn't He just be able to do everything by virtue of His divinity?

But then it struck me—if Jesus performed miracles because He was God, why would He need to be anointed? The Scripture doesn't talk about Him using His divine power to heal. Instead, it emphasizes that He operated under the anointing of the Holy Spirit. That's something profound. It means He chose to work as a man empowered by God, setting an example for us.

Luke 3:23 tells us Jesus began His ministry at about 30 years old, and in 4:14, it's clear that He didn't do miracles before being filled with the Holy Spirit. Imagine that—God in the flesh, waiting for the Spirit's anointing to kick-start His miracle ministry. It challenges the notion that His deity alone was sufficient for His works. He had to be anointed to do the Father's work effectively.

Romans 8:3 reinforces this idea. It explains that Jesus came in the likeness of sinful flesh to condemn sin and defeat Satan in the flesh. He didn't just magically erase sin; He lived a perfect life as a man, showing us what's possible when we're in sync with God's Spirit. That's why Acts 10:38 resonates so deeply. It underscores that Jesus' earthly ministry wasn't about showing off divine power but about demonstrating how we, too, can partner with God through His Spirit.

Thinking about Acts 8:45 and 1 John 4:2, I see a consistent message: Jesus was fully God and fully man. His divinity didn't nullify His humanity; instead, it was through His humanity that He operated in the power of the Spirit. That's why His miracles weren't just displays of power; they were acts of compassion and faith. Jesus healed not because He flexed divine muscle, but because He aligned Himself completely with the Father's will.

There's a story that illustrates this perfectly. Remember the man at the pool (John 5)? Everyone came to Jesus, but He approached only one—someone who, despite his circumstances, had faith to believe in healing. Jesus didn't force Himself on anyone; He responded to faith and compassionately met needs.

So, when I think about Acts 10:38 now, it's not just about Jesus' ministry; it's about how He modeled a life surrendered to God's Spirit. He didn't need to be anointed for His own sake but to show us the way—

to demonstrate that the power to do God's work comes through relationship and alignment with the Holy Spirit.

Understanding this changes everything. It means I can't just rely on my own strength or intellect but must seek God's Spirit to empower me as Jesus was empowered. It's about partnership, about living as Jesus did—fully dependent on the Father and sensitive to the Spirit's leading. That's the challenge and the invitation—to live as Jesus did, anointed by the Spirit to do the works of the Father.

The *humanity* SIDE

When I think about Jesus, the first thing that often comes to mind is His divinity. After all, He's portrayed as the Son of God, performing miracles, and speaking with authority. But recently, I've been drawn to explore His humanity more deeply. It's easy to overlook because His divine nature tends to overshadow everything else. Yet, understanding His humanity is crucial—it's what makes His life relatable and His teachings tangible.

In Acts 10:38, it says Jesus was anointed by the Holy Spirit to do good works. That phrase caught my attention because it implies a dependency on the Spirit—an aspect of humanity, not just divinity. If Jesus performed miracles solely because He was God, why would He need the Spirit's anointing? It made me realize that Jesus didn't come to show off His divine powers; He came to show us how to live in perfect harmony with God. He set aside His divine privileges to experience life as we do, relying on the Spirit's guidance and empowerment.

Luke 3:23 and 4:14 mark the beginning of Jesus' ministry after He was filled with the Holy Spirit. It's fascinating to think that for about 30 years, Jesus lived an ordinary life, growing up like any other human

THE HUMANITY SIDE

being. He didn't perform signs and wonders until the Spirit came upon Him. This shows me that His miracles weren't just demonstrations of power; they were acts of obedience and submission to the Father's will. Jesus didn't rely on His divine status to bypass the human experience; instead, He fully embraced it.

Romans 8:3 deepens this perspective by explaining that Jesus came in the likeness of sinful flesh to condemn sin and defeat Satan. This wasn't a distant victory won from a heavenly throne; it was a gritty, hands-on battle fought in the trenches of human existence. Jesus faced every temptation and trial that we do, yet He triumphed without sinning. It's through His humanity that He could truly understand our struggles and offer us a way out—a path to redemption and restoration.

Reflecting on Acts 8:45 and 1 John 4:2, I see how Jesus' humanity intersects with His divinity. Yes, He was God in the flesh, but He chose to experience life on earth just as we do. He felt hunger, fatigue, and sorrow. He laughed, cried, and formed deep friendships. He didn't come to flaunt His divinity but to demonstrate God's love and grace in a tangible, relatable way. His miracles weren't about showcasing His power; they were about revealing God's kingdom and inviting us to participate in it.

One story that encapsulates this beautifully is the healing of the paralytic (Mark 2:1-12). Here, Jesus not only heals the man physically but also forgives his sins. It's a powerful reminder that Jesus came not just to fix our external problems but to address the deepest needs of our hearts. He didn't come as a distant deity but as a compassionate Saviour who walked among us, touching lives and transforming hearts with His love.

Understanding the humanity of Jesus Christ changes how I see my own life and struggles. It reassures me that Jesus understands my weaknesses because He experienced them Himself. He didn't just sympathize from a distance; He empathizes intimately. And just as He

JESUS: MY ROLE MODEL

relied on the Holy Spirit for strength and guidance, so can I. His life becomes a model of how to live in communion with God, dependent on His Spirit, and obedient to His will.

Exploring the humanity of Christ has deepened my faith and enriched my relationship with Him. It's not about diminishing His divinity but appreciating the depth of His sacrifice and the breadth of His love. Jesus, fully God and fully human, invites us into a relationship where we can experience His grace and power in our everyday lives. As I continue on this journey of faith, I'm grateful for the example Jesus set and the promise of His presence with me, empowering me to live as He did—fully surrendered to God and filled with His Spirit.

Jesus Christ, the eternal God, embarked on a remarkable journey when He chose to become human. It's something I've pondered deeply, especially as I've delved into passages like Galatians 4:4, which states that He was born of a woman at the appointed time. This wasn't just a symbolic act or a temporary transformation—He fully embraced humanity to fulfill a divine purpose. As 1 Timothy 1:15 tells us, He entered the world to save sinners, stepping into our human experience with a mission of redemption.

Before His incarnation, Jesus existed as God, beyond the confines of time and space. He wasn't human during His appearances in the Old Testament; those were manifestations where He revealed glimpses of His glory and interacted with humanity in unique ways. However, everything changed when He "*became flesh*," as John 1:14 beautifully describes. This event, known as the Incarnation, marks the pivotal moment when the eternal Word took on human form, uniting divine nature with human flesh.

Imagine the enormity of this decision—God, who transcends all creation, willingly limiting Himself to the constraints of human existence. He didn't just take on a body; He assumed a complete human nature, with a body and a soul. He experienced the same physical

THE HUMANITY SIDE

sensations and emotional complexities that we do. He laughed, cried, felt hunger, and experienced fatigue. This wasn't a mere act of empathy but a profound demonstration of His love and solidarity with us.

As a male, Jesus began His earthly life as a vulnerable baby. He didn't arrive in a blaze of divine glory but entered quietly into a world in need of salvation. He grew up like any other child, learning and maturing through each stage of life. He didn't skip over the challenges and joys of human development but fully immersed Himself in every aspect of our human experience.

Reflecting on these truths brings me a sense of awe and gratitude. The fact that Jesus, the God-Man, walked among us and experienced life as we do, demonstrates His deep commitment to reconcile humanity to God. His life wasn't just about teaching profound truths or performing miracles; it was about showing us what it means to live in perfect communion with the Father and to love sacrificially.

In the grand narrative of redemption, Jesus' incarnation is pivotal. It bridges the gap between God and humanity, offering us a way to be restored to Him. He didn't abandon His divinity in becoming human; rather, He revealed the fullness of God's character and purpose in a tangible, relatable form. His incarnation isn't just a historical event but a continual invitation to encounter the living God who intimately knows and understands us.

As I navigate my own journey of faith, I find comfort and inspiration in knowing that Jesus, who became a man, understands my struggles, fears, and joys. He didn't just observe humanity from a distance but entered into the messiness and beauty of human existence to bring us hope and salvation. His life challenges me to embrace my humanity fully while relying on His divine strength and grace. Jesus' incarnation isn't just a theological concept but a profound truth that shapes how I view myself, others, and God's relentless pursuit of relationship with us.

Understanding the dual nature of Jesus—fully God and fully human—has been both awe-inspiring and challenging for me. It's like trying to grasp the concept of something immense and profound, yet intimately personal. When Jesus became Man, He didn't relinquish His deity; He remained fully God while embracing humanity. This truth is foundational, yet its implications stretch beyond comprehension.

Deity, by its very nature, is omnipresent—everywhere at once. It's not confined by physical limitations or boundaries. In contrast, humanity is inherently limited; it occupies specific spaces and experiences time sequentially. This distinction is crucial because it underscores the paradox of Jesus' nature: as the Incarnate Son of God, He operated within the confines of human existence while simultaneously existing beyond them.

I often reflect on the scene at the empty tomb, where the angel proclaimed, "He is not here; He has risen!" (Matthew 28:6). It reminds me that Jesus' physical body, His human nature, was localized during His earthly ministry. Just as the ocean cannot fit into a teacup, Jesus' human form could not contain His divine essence completely. His humanity was a necessary part of His mission, allowing Him to identify with us fully and redeem us through His sacrificial death.

Today, Jesus is present with us in a profound way through His Spirit. His deity, which transcends time and space, can be experienced by believers everywhere. Through the Holy Spirit, He is with us, guiding, comforting, and empowering us to live out His teachings. This ongoing presence is a testament to the continuity of His mission and the reality of His resurrection power.

While His humanity now resides in heaven, His deity remains active and accessible to all who call upon Him. This theological concept isn't just about doctrine; it's about the assurance that Jesus, who once walked among us as a man, continues to intercede for us in His divine capacity.

THE HUMANITY SIDE

It speaks to the unfathomable depth of His love and the eternal significance of His redemptive work.

I find solace in knowing that Jesus, in His divine nature, transcends all barriers and limitations. He is not bound by time or space but freely offers Himself to us, inviting us into a relationship where His presence transforms our lives. His deity and humanity converge in a perfect union, demonstrating the infinite reach of His grace and the eternal impact of His sacrifice.

Thinking about Jesus as the Second Adam, I'm reminded of the profound significance of His incarnation. He didn't just appear in human form temporarily or symbolically; He took on a real, tangible body of flesh and bone. This truth, rooted in passages like Romans 5 and 1 Corinthians 15, highlights His role in redeeming humanity from the consequences of sin. Unlike the first Adam who brought sin into the world through disobedience, Jesus came to restore what was lost, starting with His very physical presence among us.

One aspect that stands out to me is the affirmation that Jesus was not merely a spirit. In Luke 24:39, He explicitly states, "*A spirit does not have flesh and bones as you see that I have.*" This declaration challenges any notion that His physical appearance was an illusion or ethereal. His body was real, capable of experiencing all the joys and pains of human existence.

The necessity of Jesus taking on a human body becomes even clearer when considering the nature of deity. Deity, being pure Spirit, cannot die. Jesus, in His divine essence, is immortal and eternal. Yet, for the purpose of our salvation, He willingly assumed a mortal body so that He could suffer and die on our behalf. Hebrews 2 underscores this point, emphasizing that Jesus didn't come to save angels but humans—those made in the image of God and marred by sin.

JESUS: MY ROLE MODEL

The phrase "*the Word became flesh*" from John 1:14 resonates deeply with me. It encapsulates the mystery and majesty of the Incarnation—that the eternal Word, who existed from the beginning with God, took on the frailty and vulnerability of human flesh. This truth stands in stark contrast to the heresies of early Gnostics who denied the goodness of physical existence. They argued that flesh was inherently evil, leading them to reject the reality of Jesus' physical body. However, 1 John 4:2-3 confronts and rebukes this false teaching, affirming that Jesus indeed came in the flesh, fully human and fully divine.

Contemplating the humanity of Jesus means acknowledging His physicality in every sense. His body was like ours in every way except tainted by sin. Unlike us, His body was never sick and bore no scars until the crucifixion. Yet, He experienced the full range of human experiences—He grew from infancy to adulthood, He needed haircuts, He ate and drank, He slept and grew tired. These details paint a vivid picture of Jesus' complete immersion into human life, demonstrating His willingness to identify with us in every aspect.

One particular fact is that Jesus had blood, untainted by sin, which He shed for our atonement. This blood, as Hebrews 9:14 describes, cleanses our consciences from dead works to serve the living God. His physical sacrifice on the cross wasn't just symbolic; it was a tangible act of love and redemption that forever altered the course of human history.

Reflecting on these truths deepens my appreciation for Jesus' humanity. His willingness to take on flesh underscores His profound love and commitment to reconcile us to God. His physical presence among us reminds me that He understands our struggles intimately and offers us a path to redemption through His own body and blood. Jesus' human body isn't just a historical detail; it's a crucial aspect of His saving work and an invitation to embrace His love more fully.

Jesus' human body stands as a testament to His humility, His sacrifice, and His desire to restore what was broken by sin. As I continue

THE HUMANITY SIDE

to explore the depths of His incarnation, I'm challenged to view my own physical existence with gratitude and reverence. May we never cease to marvel at the wonder of Jesus becoming like us in every way, yet without sin, and may His example inspire us to live faithfully and wholeheartedly for Him.

The idea of Jesus having a human soul isn't just theological jargon to me; it's a profound aspect of His identity that shapes how I understand His life and ministry. Early on, I encountered misconceptions that Jesus only had a human body and a divine soul, but Scripture paints a richer picture. Jesus possessed a complete human soul, with all its faculties and dimensions. This truth resonates deeply as I reflect on passages that reveal His humanity in vivid detail.

One crucial aspect of Jesus' human soul was His mind. Like all humans, His knowledge was finite and grew over time. This is evident from passages such as Mark 13:32, where He openly states that He doesn't know the exact timing of His Second Coming. This admission challenges any notion of His omniscience during His earthly ministry. Instead, it underscores His genuine human experience of learning and growing in wisdom.

Emotions played a significant role in Jesus' life as well. He experienced the full spectrum of human feelings—joy, grief, compassion, and righteous anger. The story of Lazarus' death in John 11 illustrates this beautifully. Despite knowing He would raise Lazarus from the dead, Jesus wept alongside Mary and Martha, feeling the weight of their grief and the brokenness of a world marred by sin. His tears reveal His deep empathy and solidarity with humanity.

Jesus' human will is another aspect that stands out to me. Throughout His ministry, He demonstrated an unwavering commitment to fulfill the Father's will, even in the face of great suffering. In the Garden of Gethsemane, He prayed, *"Not My will, but Yours be done"* (Luke 22:42), illustrating His submission to God's plan of redemption.

This moment encapsulates the tension between His human desire to avoid pain and His divine mission to save humanity.

His soul encompassed other human characteristics as well—a memory that recalled past events and teachings, a conscience that guided His actions in accordance with God's moral law, and a heart that overflowed with compassion for the lost and broken. Jesus' humanity wasn't a facade or a temporary guise; it was integral to His mission to reconcile humanity to God.

Reflecting on Jesus' human soul deepens my appreciation for His sacrifice and His ability to identify with our struggles. He didn't just come to earth as a divine spectator; He immersed Himself fully in the human experience, experiencing its joys and its pains. His example challenges me to embrace my own humanity—to engage fully with my mind, emotions, will, and conscience in alignment with God's will.

Jesus' human soul reveals the depth of His love and the extent of His commitment to save us. His complete humanity makes His sacrifice on the cross all the more meaningful, bridging the gap between God and humanity in a way that only He could. May we continue to marvel at the mystery of His incarnation and find solace in His empathy and understanding of our human condition.

Thinking about Jesus' family and relationships brings a sense of connection and wonder. Joseph, often referred to as His step-father, played a significant role in His upbringing. Growing up, Jesus worked alongside Joseph in their carpentry business—a trade passed down through generations. Joseph, described as a righteous man in Scripture, wasn't perfect, but he believed in Jesus as his step-son. This belief was pivotal, aligning him with God's plan for salvation through Jesus.

Jesus honoured Joseph and Mary, His earthly parents, fulfilling the Fifth Commandment to honour you father and mother (Exodus 20:12). It's evident from the Gospels that He lived in obedience to them, even

THE HUMANITY SIDE

as He grew in wisdom and stature. However, Joseph's absence in Jesus' later ministry suggests he likely passed away before then, as he isn't mentioned beyond the childhood narratives in Luke 2. Jesus' commitment to Mary is touching; He entrusted her care to His beloved disciple, John, from the cross (John 19:26-27).

Mary, Jesus' mother, holds a special place in Christian theology as the virgin who gave birth to the Son of God through the Holy Spirit. Her role in the Incarnation was unique and sacred. However, Scripture also portrays her as a human who, like all of us, needed a Saviour (Luke 1:47). She wasn't sinless and didn't ascend physically into Heaven, contrary to some traditions. Mary had other children with Joseph—four half-brothers and at least two half-sisters, mentioned in Matthew 13:55-56, who initially didn't believe in Jesus until after His resurrection.

Jesus' familial relationships offer a glimpse into His humanity and the depth of His mission. Despite His earthly family having doubts at times, Jesus' spiritual family extends to all who believe in Him. In Matthew 12:50, He declares that true believers are His brothers and sisters, emphasizing the spiritual bond formed through faith in Him. Furthermore, Hebrews 2:13 portrays believers as His children, united with Him in a familial relationship that transcends earthly ties.

Moreover, the imagery of Jesus as the Bridegroom and believers as His bride, found in Ephesians 5, illustrates the intimate union between Christ and His Church. This metaphor underscores the deep love and sacrificial commitment Jesus has for His people, reminiscent of the marriage covenant. It's a reminder that our relationship with Jesus isn't just a theological concept but a personal, intimate connection rooted in His love and grace.

Reflecting on Jesus' unique family dynamics challenges me to consider the depth of His humanity and the inclusivity of His kingdom. He embraced earthly relationships while pointing to the greater spiritual reality of belonging to Him as His family. As I navigate my own relationships and identity in Christ, I'm encouraged by the truth that Jesus welcomes all who come to Him in faith as beloved members of His family—brothers, sisters, children, and His cherished Bride.

Jesus' family and relational dynamics reveal His deep love and purpose in bridging the gap between God and humanity. His earthly life provides a glimpse into His human experience, while His spiritual life invites us into a transformative relationship with Him. May we continually marvel at the beauty of being part of Jesus' family and live out our faith in response to His boundless love.

As I sit quietly, reflecting on the life and trials of Jesus, I find myself profoundly moved by His humanity. It's easy to think of Jesus as distant and divine, a figure enshrined in holy texts and lofty sermons. But when I delve deeper into His story, I discover a man who experienced life in all its complexity and who walked a path that resonates deeply with my own human experiences. This conclusion is a journey through the facets of Jesus' humanity that have touched my heart and transformed my understanding of what it means to be truly human.

I often think of Jesus as the compassionate healer, moving among the people, touching the sick, and offering words of hope to the broken-hearted. His humanity shines through in the way He responded to suffering—not with indifference, but with deep empathy and a desire to heal.

Jesus was not a solitary figure; He surrounded Himself with friends and companions, sharing in their joys and sorrows. He laughed, celebrated, and wept with them. One of the most touching moments in the Gospel is when Jesus wept at the tomb of Lazarus, His friend. Even though He knew He would raise Lazarus from the dead, He allowed Himself to feel the pain of loss and to grieve.

This aspect of Jesus' humanity speaks to me on a personal level. It reminds me that it's okay to feel deeply, to grieve, and to seek comfort

THE HUMANITY SIDE

in the company of friends. Jesus' example encourages me to build meaningful relationships, to be a source of support for others, and to let them be a source of strength for me in my times of need.

I am often struck by the story of Jesus in the wilderness, where He faced temptation. The idea that Jesus, the Son of God, could be tempted is a profound testament to His humanity. He faced hunger, loneliness, and the allure of power, yet He remained steadfast.

The most poignant aspect of Jesus' humanity is His suffering. In the Garden of Gethsemane, He experienced deep anguish, knowing the pain and betrayal that awaited Him. He prayed earnestly, even asking if the cup could pass from Him. This moment of vulnerability is a powerful reminder that Jesus understands my pain and fears.

Ultimately, the humanity of Jesus is most vividly displayed in His act of love on the cross. He willingly laid down His life, not just as a divine sacrifice, but as a man who felt every lash, every nail, and every agonizing breath. This ultimate act of love is a profound expression of His humanity and His deep love for each one of us.

As I reflect on His sacrifice, I am overwhelmed with gratitude. Jesus' humanity shows me the depth of God's love and the lengths He will go to restore and redeem us. It inspires me to live a life of love, to forgive, to serve, and to lay down my own life for others in big and small ways.

Jesus' humanity didn't end with His death; it culminated in His resurrection, a testament to the victory of life over death, hope over despair. His resurrection body, real and tangible, offers a glimpse of what lies beyond this life. It's a promise that my humanity, with all its imperfections, is part of a greater story of redemption and renewal.

Reflecting on Jesus' humanity fills me with hope. It assures me that my struggles, my pain, and even my death are not the end of the story.

There is a promise of resurrection, a future where I will be fully healed, fully alive, and fully in the presence of a loving God.

The humanity of Jesus is a powerful reminder that God is not distant and detached, but intimately involved in our lives. Jesus walked among us, felt our pain, celebrated our joys, and offered His life as a testament to God's love. His humanity invites me to live with compassion, to embrace my own humanity, and to find hope in the promise of resurrection. As I reflect on His life, I am inspired to follow His example, to love deeply, to serve faithfully, and to live with the hope and joy that comes from knowing that I am loved by the One who understands my every need and has walked the path of humanity before me.

THE HUMANITY SIDE

THE *earth* WALK

When I think about Jesus' earthly walk, it's not just a historical account or a distant theological concept—it's a journey that resonates deeply with me on a personal level. Growing up, I heard stories of Jesus walking the dusty roads of ancient in Israel, teaching crowds, performing miracles, and ultimately offering Himself as a sacrifice for humanity's redemption. These narratives weren't just tales; they were windows into the life of a man who changed everything.

Jesus' earthly walk began with humble origins in Bethlehem, where He was born to Mary and Joseph. His birth, foretold centuries earlier, marked the beginning of a life that would forever alter the course of human history. The familiar scenes of the manger and the shepherds speak of a Saviour who entered the world not in grandeur but in simplicity, identifying with the lowliest of humanity from the outset.

As He grew, Jesus didn't stay hidden in obscurity. His life unfolded in Nazareth, where He spent His childhood and early adulthood, working alongside Joseph in the carpentry trade. Imagine Him crafting wood into useful tools, labouring under the hot sun. It's in these everyday moments that I see His humanity shining through—learning, growing, and experiencing life just like any of us.

The Gospels portray Jesus not as a distant deity but as a relatable figure who walked among ordinary people, sharing their joys and sorrows. He laughed with friends at weddings, wept at the tomb of a beloved friend, and felt compassion for the crowds who followed Him seeking hope and healing. His interactions weren't scripted; they were genuine expressions of love and empathy that touched the lives of everyone He encountered.

One of the most compelling aspects of Jesus' earthly walk is His ministry. For three years, He travelled throughout Galilee and Judea, proclaiming the kingdom of God and demonstrating its reality through miraculous signs and wonders. His teachings challenged religious norms and societal expectations, offering a radical vision of God's kingdom characterized by grace, forgiveness, and inclusivity.

In contemplating Jesus' earthly walk, I'm struck by His unwavering commitment to fulfill His mission. He didn't come to be served but to serve, pouring out His life for others without reservation. His journey culminated in Jerusalem, where He willingly faced betrayal, rejection, and ultimately, death on a cross. Yet, His death wasn't the end of the story—it was the climax of a divine plan to reconcile humanity to God through His sacrificial love.

Reflecting on Jesus' earthly walk isn't just about understanding history or theology; it's about encountering a person who invites me into a deeper relationship with Him. His life challenges me to follow His example of humility, compassion, and obedience to the Father's will. As I delve into the stories of His earthly ministry, I'm reminded that His walk wasn't just for a distant past but continues to impact and transform lives today, including mine.

JESUS: MY ROLE MODEL

When I think about Jesus' time on earth, one of the most captivating aspects is His ministry of healing, signs, and wonders. These weren't just extraordinary events recorded in ancient texts; they were tangible demonstrations of God's power and compassion unfolding in real time. As I delve into the Gospels, I'm struck by the profound impact these miraculous acts had on the lives of those who witnessed them—and continue to have on us today.

Jesus' ministry of healing was transformative. He didn't just heal physical ailments; He brought restoration and hope to individuals who had been suffering for years. I imagine the scene by the pool of Bethesda, where a paralyzed man lay among the sick, waiting for someone to help him into the water. Jesus approached him with a simple question—"Do you want to be healed?" (John 5:6)—and in an instant, the man who had been unable to walk for thirty-eight years stood up, healed by the power of Jesus' words.

The stories of Jesus healing the blind, the lame, and those afflicted with various diseases resonate with me because they reveal His heart for the broken and marginalized. In Capernaum, He encountered a leper who begged to be made clean. Moved with compassion, Jesus touched him and said, *"Be clean!"* (Mark 1:41), instantly restoring his health and dignity. These acts of healing weren't merely displays of power; they were expressions of God's love breaking into human suffering.

Signs and wonders accompanied Jesus' ministry, underscoring His authority over nature and the spiritual realm. The calming of the storm on the Sea of Galilee (Mark 4:35-41) stands out to me as a vivid example of His mastery over creation. In a moment of chaos and fear, Jesus spoke a word, and the wind and waves obeyed Him. This miraculous event revealed not only His power but also His disciples' growing realization of His divine identity.

Jesus' ability to perform signs and wonders wasn't limited to physical healing and natural phenomena; He also demonstrated authority over spiritual forces. In Capernaum, He encountered a man possessed by an unclean spirit, whose life had been tormented for years. With a command, "Be silent and come out of him!" (Mark 1:25), Jesus liberated the man from demonic oppression, showcasing His authority over the spiritual realm.

These extraordinary acts of healing, signs, and wonders weren't performed for spectacle but to reveal God's kingdom breaking into our broken world. Each miracle pointed to a greater truth—that Jesus is the Son of God, the long-awaited Messiah who came to bring salvation and restoration to all who believe. His ministry challenges me to trust in His power and compassion, knowing that He is still at work in our lives today, bringing healing and hope amidst our own struggles and challenges.

Reflecting on Jesus' earthly ministry of healing, signs, and wonders deepens my faith and stirs my heart with gratitude. His willingness to touch the untouchable, heal the sick, and restore the broken speaks volumes about His character and mission. As I continue to explore these accounts, I'm reminded that Jesus' ministry wasn't confined to a specific time and place—it continues to impact and transform lives, including mine, as I place my trust in Him who is able to do immeasurably more than all we ask or imagine (Ephesians 3:20).

As I ponder the life of Jesus, one aspect stands out above all—the fact that He lived a completely sinless life. This isn't just a theological point; it's the cornerstone of His mission to reconcile humanity to God. In 1 Peter 2:22, the apostle Peter affirms that Jesus *"committed no sin, neither was deceit found in His mouth."* This declaration resonates deeply because it underscores Jesus' perfect obedience to God's will in every thought, word, and action.

Hebrews 4:15 further emphasizes the significance of Jesus' sinlessness. It declares that Jesus *"in every respect has been tempted as we are, yet without sin."* This verse portrays Jesus as the ultimate high

JESUS: MY ROLE MODEL

priest who can sympathize with our weaknesses because He faced the same temptations we do, yet He never succumbed to sin. His sinlessness wasn't due to a lack of exposure to temptation but stemmed from His unwavering commitment to righteousness.

The apostle Paul reinforces this truth in 2 Corinthians 5:21, proclaiming that Jesus *"knew no sin."* This succinct statement encapsulates the purity of Jesus' character and the necessity of His sinlessness for the accomplishment of our salvation. Had Jesus sinned even once, He would have been disqualified from serving as the sacrificial Lamb for humanity's sins. The Old Testament requirement for the Passover lamb to be without blemish, as stated in Exodus 12, finds its ultimate fulfillment in Jesus as the spotless Lamb of God.

The sinlessness of Jesus isn't just a theological abstraction but a practical reality with profound implications. It means that His sacrifice on the cross was not only sufficient but perfect. His death wasn't the tragic end of a righteous life; it was the culmination of a divine plan to redeem humanity from the bondage of sin. Jesus willingly offered Himself as the perfect atoning sacrifice, satisfying God's justice and extending His mercy to all who believe.

Reflecting on Jesus' sinlessness challenges me to confront my own shortcomings and inadequacies. Unlike Jesus, I am prone to sin and fall short of God's glory (Romans 3:23). Yet, His sinless life offers me hope and assurance. Through His death and resurrection, He provides forgiveness and reconciliation with God, inviting me into a restored relationship marked by grace and mercy.

The sinlessness of Jesus isn't merely a theological concept but a foundational truth that shapes my understanding of salvation and discipleship. His perfect obedience and sacrificial death demonstrate God's boundless love for humanity and His desire to bring us back into communion with Him. May we continually marvel at the sinlessness of

Jesus and respond with gratitude and faith, trusting in His finished work on the cross for our redemption.

When I reflect on Jesus's ministry, the verse from Hebrews 13:8 immediately comes to mind: "*Jesus Christ is the same yesterday, and today, and forever.*" This powerful statement encapsulates the enduring nature of His ministry—consistent, unwavering, and eternally relevant across time and cultures.

One of the remarkable aspects of Christ's ministry is its relevance across generations. His teachings on love, forgiveness, and justice continue to challenge and inspire people from diverse backgrounds and cultures. Whether addressing a crowd on a hillside in ancient Israel or speaking to hearts through Scripture today, Jesus' words penetrate to the core of human existence, offering timeless wisdom and guidance.

Moreover, Jesus' ministry transcends mere historical record; it speaks directly to my life and circumstances. His promise to be with us always, even to the end of the age (Matthew 28:20), assures me of His presence and guidance in every season of life. As I navigate challenges, uncertainties, and joys, His unchanging ministry provides a steadfast anchor—a source of hope and strength that never fails.

The consistency of Christ's ministry also extends to His unchanging role as Saviour and Redeemer. He came to seek and to save the lost (Luke 19:10), offering salvation freely to all who repent and believe in Him. His sacrificial death on the cross and victorious resurrection demonstrate His power over sin and death, securing eternal life for those who trust in Him.

Reflecting on Christ's unchanging ministry challenges me to live with the same steadfast commitment and devotion to His teachings. His example of selfless love and servant leadership inspires me to follow Him wholeheartedly, seeking to embody His compassion and grace in my interactions with others. As I grow in my relationship with Him, I am reminded that His ministry isn't confined to the past or present—it continues to transform lives and renew hearts today and will do so for eternity.

Hebrews 13:8 serves as a profound reminder of the enduring impact of Christ's ministry. His teachings, His miracles, and His love remain as powerful and relevant today as they were during His earthly ministry. May we continue to embrace His unchanging truth, find solace in His unending grace, and proclaim His unshakable kingdom to a world in need of His saving love.

Jesus's ministry of compassion and miraculous healing remains as potent and relevant today as it was two thousand years ago. The words from Matthew 12:15 echo in my mind, reminding me that "many followed him, and he healed all their sick." This simple yet profound statement speaks volumes about Jesus' unwavering commitment to meeting the needs of those who came to Him in faith.

Throughout the Gospels, we see numerous accounts of Jesus' healing touch transforming lives. Matthew 14:36 tells us that "*all who touched him were healed*," emphasizing the immediate and complete restoration that came to those who reached out to Him in faith. In Luke 6:19, we witness crowds pressing in to touch Jesus because power emanated from Him, healing them all. These passages paint a vivid picture of Jesus' limitless compassion and supernatural ability to heal.

The assurance that Jesus excludes no one from His healing touch is a powerful encouragement. In Matthew 8:16, we read how "many who were demon-possessed were brought to him, and he drove out the spirits with a word and healed all the sick." The inclusivity of His ministry extends to all who are afflicted—no sickness, no condition is beyond His ability to restore. Luke 4:40 reinforces this truth, recounting how "all who had various kinds of sickness" were brought to Jesus, and He healed each one with the laying on of hands.

THE EARTH WALK

Acts 10:38 provides further insight into the source of Jesus' healing power. It affirms that "*God anointed Jesus of Nazareth with the Holy Spirit and power,*" enabling Him to go about "doing good and healing all who were under the power of the devil." This divine anointing underscores Jesus' authority over sickness and oppression, demonstrating that His healing ministry is rooted in God's presence and purpose.

Reflecting on these passages fills me with faith and expectation. The same Jesus who healed the sick and delivered the oppressed in Bible days is alive and active today. His power to heal physical, mentally, psychologically, deliver from spiritual bondage, and restore broken lives remains unchanged.

He invites us to approach Him with boldness and trust, believing that His compassion and healing touch are available to all who seek Him.

In conclusion, Christ the Healer stands as a beacon of hope and restoration for all humanity. His ministry of healing transcends time and circumstance, offering comfort and wholeness to those who come to Him in faith. As I embrace His unchanging promise to heal and deliver, I am reminded that His love knows no bounds and His power knows no limits. May we, like those who came to Him in the Gospels, reach out and touch Him in faith, confident that He will heal us completely and compassionately, for He is the same yesterday, today, and forever.

IN *the* GARDEN

When I think about Jesus in the garden before His crucifixion, a profound sense of solemnity and significance fills my heart. This momentous event, captured vividly in the Gospels, reveals the depth of Jesus' humanity and the weight of His divine mission. As I reflect on this pivotal night, I am drawn into the garden of Gethsemane, where Jesus wrestled in prayer with the impending ordeal that lay ahead.

The garden of Gethsemane holds a special place in the narrative of Jesus' final hours. It was here, amidst the quiet of olive trees and the soft rustle of leaves, that Jesus poured out His heart to the Father. The Gospel of Matthew paints a poignant picture of Jesus' anguish, describing how He "*began to be sorrowful and troubled*" (Matthew 26:37). This wasn't merely fear of physical pain; it was the weight of humanity's sin and the looming separation from the Father that He faced on the cross.

As Jesus knelt in prayer, His soul was "overwhelmed with sorrow to the point of death" (Matthew 26:38). Luke's Gospel adds that His sweat fell like drops of blood, a rare medical condition known as hematidrosis brought on by extreme emotional distress (Luke 22:44). In this moment of intense vulnerability, Jesus exemplified the depth of His humanity,

IN THE GARDEN

experiencing the full range of human emotions while willingly submitting to the Father's will.

The significance of Jesus' prayer in the garden extends beyond a personal struggle; it reveals His unwavering obedience and love for humanity. Despite His anguish, Jesus prayed, *"Father, if you are willing, take this cup from me; yet not my will, but yours be don*e" (Luke 22:42). This prayer encapsulates His submission to the divine plan of redemption—His willingness to endure the cross for the sake of reconciling humanity to God.

In contemplating Jesus' agonizing prayer in the garden, I am confronted with the depth of His love and sacrifice. His willingness to drink the cup of suffering and face the horrors of crucifixion on our behalf underscores the magnitude of His mission. As I stand with Jesus in the garden through the pages of Scripture, I am reminded of His profound love for me and His unwavering commitment to fulfill God's plan of salvation.

Jesus' prayer in the garden of Gethsemane reveals His humanity and divinity in perfect harmony. It invites me to consider the cost of my salvation and to respond with gratitude and surrender to His sacrificial love. As I journey through the events leading to the cross, may I never forget the significance of Jesus' prayer in the garden—a poignant reminder of His ultimate act of love that brings hope and redemption to all who believe.

The night Jesus was betrayed marked the culmination of a long, eventful day that began with the Passover meal shared with His disciples. I can imagine the atmosphere in the upper room—Jesus breaking bread, sharing the cup, and solemnly explaining the significance of His impending sacrifice. Little did they know, and perhaps even He fully comprehended, the weight of what was to come that very night.

JESUS: MY ROLE MODEL

As Jesus withdrew to the Garden of Gethsemane with Peter, James, and John, the heaviness of His impending ordeal descended upon Him like a dark cloud. The writer of Hebrews provides a glimpse into this profound moment, describing how Jesus offered up prayers and supplications with loud cries and tears to His Father (Hebrews 5:7). This wasn't a mere formality; it was a deep, agonizing communion with the Father as Jesus grappled with the path laid before Him.

In the solitude of the garden, Jesus' anguish was palpable. Luke's Gospel vividly portrays His distress, noting that His sweat became like drops of blood falling to the ground (Luke 22:44). This rare medical phenomenon, hematidrosis, speaks to the intensity of His emotional and spiritual struggle. Jesus, fully aware of the impending separation from the Father and the weight of humanity's sin, pleaded with His disciples to watch and pray with Him (Mark 14:34).

The gravity of Jesus' prayers in Gethsemane reflects His deep humanity and profound obedience to the Father's will. Three times He prayed, each time surrendering to God's plan while wrestling with the agony of what lay ahead. In His humanity, Jesus questioned the necessity of His impending suffering, yet in perfect submission, He entrusted Himself to the Father's purpose (Luke 22:42).

Before His final prayer, an angel appeared to strengthen Him—an act of divine compassion amidst His anguish (Luke 22:43). Yet, Jesus faced the full weight of sin's misery and shame. He bore the burden of humanity's guilt and despair, anticipating the moment on the cross when He would cry out, "*My God, my God, why have you forsaken me?*" (Matthew 27:46).

The agony Jesus experienced wasn't merely physical or emotional; it was the anticipation of taking on the sins of the world. Unlike us, who are not spotless lambs, Jesus was sinless and pure. His journey from His public ministry, marked by miracles and teachings, to the imminent cross meant bearing the full weight of humanity's sin and separation

IN THE GARDEN

from the Father. It was a transition from demonstrating His power to laying down His life as the ultimate sacrifice.

In our own lives, we often face challenges and uncertainties. When we encounter sickness or hardship, we may wonder if it is God's will to heal or provide. However, Jesus' journey through Gethsemane reveals a different perspective. He willingly submitted to the Father's will, even when it meant facing agony and forsakenness. His prayer in Matthew 26:39—"My Father, if it is possible, may this cup be taken from me"—demonstrates His humanity and the depth of His struggle.

Despite His plea, "*Yet not as I will, but as you will,*" God did not answer Jesus' request to remove the cup of suffering (Matthew 26:39). This moment challenges me to reconsider my own prayers and expectations. Jesus, though perfect and without sin, submitted to God's greater plan, even when His heartfelt desire seemed at odds with it. It reminds me that prayer isn't about manipulating God's will but aligning my heart with His, trusting His wisdom and sovereignty.

Moreover, Jesus' experience in Gethsemane highlights the reality of temptation. It's not a sin to be tempted; rather, sin enters when we yield to temptation and act contrary to God's will. In His agony, Jesus faced the temptation to avoid the cross, yet He remained obedient to God's plan. His example encourages me to resist temptation and to trust God's purposes, even when they lead through valleys of uncertainty and pain.

Jesus' agony in the Garden of Gethsemane marks a pivotal moment in His ministry—a transition from triumph to sacrificial surrender. His willingness to endure suffering and death demonstrates His unfathomable love for humanity. As I reflect on His prayerful submission and unwavering obedience, I am inspired to trust God's plan for my life, knowing that His purposes are perfect and His grace is sufficient, even in moments of deepest anguish.

John 10:17-18 underscores Jesus' unique authority and power. He had the ability to prevent His own death, akin to someone having the means to defend themselves yet choosing to lay down their defense. Jesus willingly chose to endure suffering and death, not out of weakness or inability to resist, but out of love and obedience to fulfill God's redemptive plan for humanity.

In Matthew 26:53, Jesus affirms His sovereignty and life-giving power. He could have summoned legions of angels to defend Himself, but instead, He chose to lay down His life willingly. His restraint in the face of betrayal and injustice speaks volumes about His divine purpose—to take upon Himself the sins, sicknesses, and poverty of the world.

The depth of Jesus' obedience and sacrificial love becomes even clearer in Hebrews 5:7, which describes how He "learned obedience from what He suffered." This wasn't about learning to obey for the first time; rather, it was about experiencing the full weight of obedience in the context of suffering and temptation. Jesus' journey through Gethsemane and ultimately to the cross was a demonstration of perfect obedience to the Father's will.

What Jesus faced in Gethsemane wasn't merely physical suffering; it was the prospect of separation from God the Father, a separation that would last for three agonizing days. The intimacy they had shared for eternity would be momentarily broken as Jesus bore the sin of the world upon Himself. This separation, more than any physical pain, caused Him anguish and sorrow.

Through His obedience, Jesus completed the task set before Him. Hebrews 4:15 reassures us that Jesus, our High Priest, understands our temptations and struggles because He experienced them firsthand in His human flesh. He knows what it is like to face temptation and yet remain without sin. His life serves as the ultimate example of faithfulness and trust in God's plan, even when it leads through the valley of suffering.

IN THE GARDEN

Jesus' journey from Gethsemane to the cross is a profound testament to His sacrificial love and obedience. He willingly embraced the fullness of human experience, including temptation, so that He could empathize with us and intercede on our behalf as our High Priest. As I contemplate His obedience and selflessness, I am reminded of the depth of God's love for us and challenged to surrender my own will to His, trusting in His wisdom and sovereignty over my life.

Hebrews 2:17-18 and Hebrews 4:15-16 provide a framework for understanding why Jesus endured such anguish. He willingly entered into our human experience, facing every temptation and trial that we encounter. This wasn't an abstract notion; it was a lived reality. Jesus, fully God and fully man, experienced the full range of human emotions and challenges, yet without sin.

In the Garden, Jesus' prayerful struggle revealed His complete identification with humanity. He didn't just sympathize with our weaknesses; He intimately understood them because He had walked in our shoes. His agony wasn't merely about the physical suffering that awaited Him on the cross; it was about the spiritual and emotional weight of bearing the sins of the world.

The purpose of Jesus' suffering in the Garden was twofold. First, it demonstrated His perfect obedience to the Father's will. Despite His natural human desire to avoid the cross, Jesus submitted Himself completely, saying, *"Not my will, but yours be done"* (Luke 22:42). In doing so, He modeled for us what true surrender and trust in God look like, even in the face of unimaginable pain.

Secondly, Jesus' agony in Gethsemane was a profound act of solidarity with humanity. He knew that His sacrifice was necessary to redeem us from sin and reconcile us to God. By experiencing temptation and suffering firsthand, Jesus became our sympathetic High Priest, able to intercede for us and offer us grace and mercy in our time of need (Hebrews 4:15-16).

As I ponder the purpose of Jesus' agony in the Garden, I am reminded of His incredible love for each one of us. He willingly endured the anguish and temptation so that we could have forgiveness, healing, and eternal life. His journey from Gethsemane to the cross was paved with selflessness and sacrifice, demonstrating the depth of God's love and the extent of His redemption plan.

Today, Jesus continues to intercede for us before the Father, understanding our weaknesses and offering us grace to overcome temptation. His example challenges me to trust in God's plan for my life, even when it leads through difficult circumstances. May we draw near to Him, knowing that He understands our struggles intimately and offers us His strength and peace to persevere.

•

IN THE GARDEN

THE TRIAL

As I reflect on the trial of Jesus, I am deeply moved by Jesus' profound act of self-sacrifice. Jesus, the Son of God, faced unjust accusations, mockery, and betrayal leading up to His crucifixion. His trial was a stark contrast to the love and compassion He had shown throughout His ministry. Yet, in the midst of His suffering, Jesus demonstrated a love that surpasses understanding—a love that compelled Him to lay down His life for His friends.

The events leading to Jesus' trial began with His arrest in the Garden of Gethsemane. Despite knowing the agony and betrayal that awaited Him, Jesus willingly surrendered Himself to the authorities. As He stood before Pilate and the religious leaders, false accusations were hurled at Him, yet He remained silent, fulfilling the prophecy that He would be led like a lamb to the slaughter (Isaiah 53:7).

During His trial, Jesus endured physical and emotional abuse. He was mocked, spat upon, and struck repeatedly. Pilate, torn between justice and appeasing the crowd, questioned Jesus about His identity and intentions. In John 18:37, Jesus declared, *"For this I came into the world, to testify to the truth. Everyone on the side of truth listens to me."*

His words resonated with me, revealing His unwavering commitment to His mission—even unto death.

The heart-wrenching moment came when Pilate offered to release either Jesus or Barabbas, a notorious criminal. The crowd, manipulated by the religious leaders, chose to release Barabbas and demanded Jesus' crucifixion. Pilate, though finding no fault in Jesus, yielded to the crowd's demands, symbolically washing his hands of the decision. In that pivotal moment, Jesus bore the weight of humanity's sin and rejection, willingly laying down His life for His friends, including those who condemned Him.

As I contemplate Jesus' trial, I'm confronted with a challenging question: Can I, like Jesus, lay down my life for my friends? Jesus taught, *"Greater love has no one than this: to lay down one's life for one's friends"* (John 15:13). His sacrificial love sets a standard that transcends cultural norms and personal comfort. It calls me to consider how I can selflessly serve and sacrifice for others, even when it's difficult or unpopular.

In my own life, laying down my life for others may not involve physical martyrdom, but it requires daily acts of kindness, forgiveness, and compassion. It means putting others' needs before my own, extending grace to those who hurt me, and standing up for justice and truth, even when it's challenging. Jesus' example challenges me to examine my priorities and motivations, urging me to live a life marked by sacrificial love and service.

Ultimately, Jesus' trial and crucifixion were not the end of the story. His death on the cross paved the way for redemption and reconciliation between God and humanity. Through His resurrection, Jesus conquered sin and death, offering eternal life to all who believe in Him. His sacrifice serves as a powerful reminder of the depth of God's love for us and His desire for us to love one another sacrificially.

JESUS: MY ROLE MODEL

As I strive to follow Jesus' example of laying down my life for my friends, I am reminded of the profound impact His love has had on my own life. May His sacrificial love continue to inspire and empower me to live a life that reflects His grace and truth in every circumstance.

As I delve into the chronology of Jesus' trial, I am struck by the swift and tumultuous events that unfolded, leading to His crucifixion. Each moment, meticulously recorded in Scripture, reveals the profound purpose behind His unjust condemnation and ultimate sacrifice for humanity.

The night of Jesus' betrayal in the Garden of Gethsemane marked the beginning of His trial. Matthew 26 recounts how Jesus was apprehended and brought before Annas, the former high priest, for questioning. From there, He was swiftly taken to Caiaphas, the current high priest, and the Jewish council (John 18:12). Amidst the darkness of night, Peter's denial of Jesus foreshadowed the impending trials and turmoil that would follow (John 18:24).

Luke 22:66 details the assembly of the Jewish council, where false witnesses accused Jesus of blasphemy and sedition. Despite the lack of credible evidence, the religious leaders sought to condemn Him to death. Meanwhile, the treachery of Judas Iscariot reached its tragic conclusion as he succumbed to guilt and despair, ending his own life by hanging himself (Matthew 27:3).

At dawn, the religious leaders brought Jesus before Pontius Pilate, the Roman governor, to secure His execution. The timing of these events was deliberate—Pilate's verdict would seal Jesus' fate. The purpose of Jesus' trial was not merely to determine His guilt or innocence under Roman law, but to fulfill a greater divine plan of redemption.

The overarching purpose of Jesus' trial was rooted in God's redemptive love for humanity. John 10:1,12 illustrates this beautifully through the imagery of Jesus as the Good Shepherd who lays down His life for His sheep. Jesus willingly endured the mockery, false accusations, and brutal treatment so that through His rejection, we could be accepted into God's family as forgiven and redeemed children.

The trial of Jesus serves as a poignant reminder of the lengths God was willing to go to reconcile us to Himself. Jesus' willingness to suffer rejection and injustice demonstrated His perfect obedience to the Father's will and His boundless love for us. His sacrifice on the cross became the ultimate atonement for our sins, providing a way for us to be reconciled to God and receive eternal life.

Reflecting on the chronology and purpose of Jesus' trial deepens my appreciation for His sacrificial love and steadfast commitment to fulfilling God's plan of salvation. It challenges me to consider how I respond to trials and injustices in my own life—whether I am willing to trust God's sovereignty and purpose, even when circumstances seem unjust or difficult.

Jesus' trial was a pivotal moment in human history, marking the beginning of His journey to the cross. It was through His rejection and suffering that God's divine purpose of salvation was accomplished.

After the agonizing prayer in the Garden of Gethsemane, Jesus faced a relentless night of interrogation, scourging, and physical abuse. He was mocked, spat upon, and beaten beyond recognition. By the time He was led to Golgotha early the next morning, He was already severely weakened, yet He bore the weight of His cross along the dusty road, stumbling under its burden.

Crucifixion, a common Roman form of execution, was designed to inflict maximum pain and humiliation. Medical experts and forensic historians have detailed the horrific process: the nailing of hands and feet, forcing the victim to push up against the cross to breathe, resulting in excruciating pain and eventual suffocation. Jesus endured this agonizing death alongside the main public highway, stripped of His clothing, exposed to the elements, and subjected to public scorn.

The gospel narratives recount that Jesus was nailed to the cross at 9 o'clock in the morning, and by 3 o'clock in the afternoon, He breathed His last breath (Mark 15:25, 33-37). On the surface, it may seem that His ordeal lasted only six hours, but there is more to the story than meets the eye. The physical suffering was only part of the profound sacrifice Jesus made on the cross.

Behind the scenes of Jesus' crucifixion lies the spiritual and theological significance of His death. Jesus, the sinless Lamb of God, willingly laid down His life to atone for the sins of humanity. His death was not just a tragic end to a life of love and compassion; it was the fulfillment of God's plan for redemption. Through His sacrifice, Jesus bore the weight of our sins, offering forgiveness and reconciliation to all who believe in Him.

For the first three hours on the cross, Jesus functioned as our Great High Priest. His intercession and mediation were evident as He bore the weight of our sins. Then, at noon, a haunting darkness descended upon the land, shrouding the scene in an eerie silence (Luke 23:44). During these hours, Jesus transitioned from High Priest to Sacrifice.

In becoming sin for us, Jesus took upon Himself the sins of the world—every lie, every betrayal, every act of hatred and injustice. He became a symbol of shame and disgrace, bearing the full weight of our collective guilt. In that moment, He experienced the unimaginable: being cut off from the fellowship with God and humanity, not just temporally but also in the eternal realm.

The work of Jesus on the cross, as completed in history, is a finished masterpiece of redemption. His sacrificial death and subsequent resurrection secured victory over sin and death. Jesus is no longer hanging on a cross; He has risen from the dead and now reigns in heaven, seated at the right hand of the Father, with all authority over the universe.

Yet, if we could peer beyond the confines of time and glimpse eternity from the heavenly perspective, we might perceive a deeper truth. In the eternal realm, where God exists outside of time, a profound mystery unfolds: the eternal Son of God, who willingly suffered on our behalf, continues to bear the scars of human sin. Though glorified in His resurrected body, the memory of His sacrificial act remains eternally significant.

From the vantage point of heaven, we might grasp the eternal implications of Jesus' sacrifice. It's not just a one-time event but an eternal reality where the Son of God, in His eternal being, bears the marks of our redemption. The suffering He endured on the cross echoes throughout eternity, a testament to His unfathomable love and the depth of His commitment to save humanity.

As I reflect on the mystery of Christ's passion, I am humbled by the enormity of God's plan for our salvation. Jesus' willingness to suffer and die for our sins transcends human understanding. It challenges me to live in awe and gratitude for His sacrificial love, knowing that His sacrifice bridged the gap between God and humanity for all eternity.

As I reflect on the crucifixion of Jesus, the details of that fateful day stand out with profound significance. It was a day like no other, marking the pinnacle of God's plan for redemption and the depths of His love for humanity.

The day began early, with Jesus being nailed to the cross at 9:00 in the morning. It was a solemn and somber moment as He willingly submitted Himself to the hands of sinful men. The executioners, hardened soldiers accustomed to death, carried out their grim task mechanically. But in that act of brutality, God's redemptive plan was unfolding.

The third hour, 9:00 am, marked the beginning of Jesus' crucifixion. It was at this hour that the weight of the world's sin began to press upon Him. The nails pierced His hands and feet, securing Him to the rough-hewn wood. Despite the pain and agony, Jesus endured it all with a steadfast resolve, knowing that His sacrifice was the only way to reconcile humanity to God.

By the sixth hour, noon, darkness descended upon the land. This supernatural darkness was not just a natural eclipse but a symbol of the cosmic significance of Jesus' death. It was a solemn darkness, reflecting the weight of sin and the separation it caused between God and humanity. In those hours of darkness, Jesus hung on the cross, bearing the sins of the world upon His shoulders.

From noon until the ninth hour, 3:00 pm, the darkness persisted. It was during these hours that Jesus endured the fullness of God's wrath against sin. The pain of crucifixion was unbearable, yet it paled in comparison to the spiritual agony Jesus experienced as He bore the separation from His Father. In that moment, He cried out in anguish, "My God, my God, why have you forsaken me?" (Matthew 27:46).

At 3:00 pm, the ninth hour, Jesus uttered His final words, "It is finished" (John 19:30). With these words, He declared that His work of redemption was complete. The veil in the temple was torn in two, symbolizing the access to God that was now open to all through faith in Christ. Jesus, the perfect Lamb of God, had fulfilled the Old Testament sacrificial system once and for all.

As I contemplate the events of that day, I am reminded of the depth of Jesus' love and the magnitude of His sacrifice. He endured six hours on the cross, bearing our sins and suffering in our place. The darkness from noon to 3:00 pm was a poignant reminder of the price Jesus paid for our redemption. His death was not just a physical act but a spiritual victory over sin and death.

THE TRIAL

Today, as I ponder the crucifixion of Jesus, I am grateful for His willingness to endure such suffering on my behalf. His death has brought me forgiveness, reconciliation with God, and eternal life.

May I never take for granted the immense sacrifice Jesus made for me. May His death on the cross always be a source of hope, assurance, and gratitude in my life, knowing that through Him, I have been redeemed and made new.

Matthew, Mark, Luke, and John, in their Gospel accounts, describe the scenes they witnessed with their own eyes. They recount the agony of Jesus, the darkness that covered the land, and the tearing of the temple veil from top to bottom. These were not mere coincidences or random occurrences; they were divine signs of the spiritual realities unfolding in the heavenly realms.

Paul, in his letter to the Galatians, sheds light on the deeper spiritual significance of Jesus' crucifixion. He addresses the Galatian believers who were being misled into legalism, reminding them that they did not witness Jesus' crucifixion firsthand because it occurred two decades earlier. He admonishes them for being foolish, indicating their senselessness in turning away from the grace of Christ to embrace the constraints of the Jewish law.

The Galatians had been bewitched, Paul asserts, as if someone had cast a spell on them. They were being persuaded to adopt practices and observances meant for Jews, not Gentiles who had found freedom in Christ. Paul emphasizes that the law was given to the Jews as a temporary measure, a tutor to lead them to Christ, but now that Christ had come, believers are no longer under the law but under grace.

The tearing of the temple veil symbolized the end of the old covenant and the opening of a new way to God through Jesus Christ. It signified that access to God was no longer restricted to the high priest and the inner sanctuary but was now available to all through faith in

Jesus' sacrificial death. This tearing was a spiritual declaration that Jesus, as the true Passover Lamb, had made the ultimate atonement for sin, once and for all.

As I meditate on these truths, I am reminded of the spiritual warfare that took place on the cross. Jesus' death was not just a physical event but a cosmic battle against sin, death, and the powers of darkness. Through His sacrifice, Jesus conquered sin and death, offering salvation and eternal life to all who believe.

On Paul's words in 2 Corinthians 3:5-6, I am reminded of the profound shift in perspective that comes with embracing the ministry of the Spirit over the ministry of the law. Paul teaches us that our sufficiency is not from ourselves but from God, who has made us competent to be ministers of a new covenant, not of the letter but of the Spirit. This new covenant is characterized not by external rules and regulations but by the internal transformation wrought by the Holy Spirit.

The law, encapsulated in the Ten Commandments, was a standard of righteousness that highlighted our shortcomings and inability to meet God's perfect standards. Yet, Paul challenges us to move beyond a legalistic adherence to these commandments and to embrace the higher law of love that Jesus taught. In Matthew 22:37-40, Jesus summarized the entire law in two commandments: to love God with all our heart, soul, and mind, and to love our neighbor as ourselves. If we truly live in love, we fulfill the righteous requirements of the law.

In 1 Corinthians 13, Paul elaborates on the supremacy of love, contrasting it with the pursuit of spiritual gifts and acts of righteousness. He emphasizes that without love, all our efforts are meaningless. Love is patient, kind, and keeps no record of wrongs. It is the foundation upon which the Christian life is built, and it transforms our walk with God and our relationships with others.

Paul's comparison between the ministry of the law and the ministry of the Spirit in 2 Corinthians 3:7-11 is striking. He describes the law as bringing death because it condemns us for our sins and shortcomings. The law, though glorious in its revelation of God's righteous standards, cannot impart life or righteousness. In contrast, the ministry of the Spirit is glorious because it brings life and righteousness through faith in Jesus Christ.

When we accept Jesus Christ as our Saviour and Lord, the veil that once obscured our understanding of God's grace and truth is lifted. This veil represents the spiritual blindness and separation from God that the law perpetuated. But through Jesus, we have direct access to God and His truth. We no longer need to rely on external laws and regulations for our righteousness because we are made righteous by faith in Christ and empowered by the Holy Spirit to live according to God's will.

In Galatians 3:1, Paul addresses the Galatian believers who were being misled into returning to legalism and the observance of Jewish customs. He reminds them of the crucifixion of Jesus Christ, urging them to remember that they were not physically present when Jesus was crucified. Yet, through Paul's preaching and their acceptance of the gospel, they have come to know and experience the power of Jesus' sacrifice for their sins. Paul emphasizes that faith in Jesus Christ, not adherence to the law, is the basis of their salvation and spiritual life.

As I ponder these teachings, I am challenged to examine my own heart and life. Have I fully embraced the ministry of the Spirit, which brings life and righteousness through faith in Jesus Christ? Am I living in the freedom and grace that Christ has provided, or am I tempted to revert to a legalistic mindset that focuses on external rules and regulations? May I continually surrender to the Holy Spirit's work in my life, allowing Him to transform me from the inside out and empower me to love God and others as Christ has loved me.

JESUS: MY ROLE MODEL

Imagine being there, in the midst of the chaos and confusion, as Jesus was dragged from one authority to another. He stood silently before His accusers, subjected to false charges and baseless accusations. The very thought of the unfairness He endured makes my heart ache. Jesus, who had done no wrong, who had healed the sick and taught about love and forgiveness, was treated as a criminal.

As I consider the trial, I am struck by the glaring injustice of it all. Pontius Pilate, the Roman governor, found no fault in Jesus, yet he bowed to the pressure of the angry mob. He washed his hands of the matter, symbolically absolving himself of responsibility, but in reality, he was complicit in the greatest miscarriage of justice the world has ever known. I can't help but feel the weight of this injustice, knowing that it was all part of God's plan for our redemption.

One of the most striking aspects of Jesus' trial is His silence. He could have defended Himself, called down angels, or spoken a word to change His fate. Instead, He chose to remain silent, like a lamb led to the slaughter. This silence wasn't a sign of weakness but a testament to His incredible strength and commitment to fulfilling His Father's will.

When I think about Jesus' silence, I am reminded of the times in my own life when I have faced accusations or misunderstandings. It's so tempting to defend myself, to argue my case, but Jesus shows me a different way. He shows me the power of trusting in God's plan, even when it doesn't make sense to the world. His silence speaks volumes about His love and His willingness to endure suffering for my sake.

Throughout Jesus's trial, He demonstrated a courage that is beyond comprehension. He faced the taunts, the beatings, and the mockery with a quiet dignity that commands my deepest respect. He was abandoned by His closest friends, betrayed by one of His disciples, and denied by another. Yet, He stood firm, knowing that this was the path He had to walk for the salvation of humanity.

THE TRIAL

As I think about the courage of Jesus, I am inspired to face my own challenges with a similar strength. Life often brings trials and tribulations, but Jesus' example encourages me to stand firm in my faith, to trust in God's plan, and to face adversity with grace and dignity.

The trial of Jesus ultimately led to the cross, where He made the ultimate sacrifice for me and for all of humanity. The weight of this realization is almost too much to bear. Jesus, the Son of God, willingly gave His life so that I might have eternal life. His trial was the prelude to the greatest act of love the world has ever known.

When I reflect on this, I am filled with a profound sense of gratitude. Jesus endured the trial, the suffering, and the cross because of His love for me. This knowledge fills me with a desire to live my life in a way that honors His sacrifice, to love others as He has loved me, and to share the message of His incredible grace with the world.

In conclusion, the trial of Jesus is a powerful reminder of His love, His sacrifice, and His victory. It is a story that touches my heart and inspires me to live with courage, faith, and gratitude. As I reflect on His trial, I am reminded of the incredible price He paid for my redemption and the hope that I have in Him. May His love and His sacrifice always be at the forefront of my mind, guiding me on my journey and inspiring me to live a life that honors Him.

THE CRUCIFIXION

As I reflect on the tumultuous events spanning from the Last Supper to the Resurrection, I am struck by the profound emotional journey Jesus and his disciples undertook during those fateful days. It was a time of intense highs and lows, of profound teachings and heartbreaking betrayals. These were the moments that ultimately defined the course of human history, where the fate of humanity hung in the balance.

The Last Supper, a poignant moment of fellowship and solemnity, stands as a testament to Jesus' deep love for his disciples. Around that table, he shared bread and wine, symbols of his impending sacrifice, and spoke words of comfort and forewarning. Little did they know, within hours, the tranquility of that evening would be shattered by the turmoil of betrayal and arrest in the Garden of Gethsemane.

In the Garden, I imagine the heaviness that must have settled over Jesus as he prayed fervently, knowing the weight of what lay ahead. The disciples, exhausted and unaware, struggled to keep watch as Jesus grappled with the impending sacrifice that would soon unfold. It was a night where fear and faith collided, and where Jesus, in his humanity,

THE CRUCIFIXION

faced the full weight of what it meant to drink from the cup his Father had given him.

The subsequent trials, the mockery, and the crucifixion depict a harrowing journey of suffering and redemption. From the halls of Pilate's judgment to the agonizing climb up Golgotha's hill, Jesus bore the weight of humanity's sin and shame upon his shoulders. The darkness that enveloped the land as he hung on the cross mirrored the spiritual battle raging beyond the visible realm.

Yet, through it all, the story does not end in despair. The Resurrection morning brings a glimmer of hope and triumph. The tomb, once sealed and guarded, now stands empty, a testament to the victory over sin and death that Jesus secured through his sacrifice. From the depths of despair to the heights of resurrection glory, this journey encapsulates the transformative power of God's love and grace.

As I delve into these pivotal moments, I am reminded of the profound impact they continue to have on my faith and understanding of God's redemption plan. The events from the Last Supper to the Resurrection are not merely historical accounts but serve as a poignant reminder of God's unending love and the hope we have in Christ. It is a journey that invites me to reflect on my own response to God's sacrificial love and to embrace the promise of new life found in Jesus Christ.

WEDNESDAY, NISAN 13

18:00 hours or 6:00 pm – (End of Tuesday – beginning of Wednesday)

As the night descended into the early hours of Wednesday, Nisan 13, the atmosphere was charged with a mix of anticipation and tension. The disciples of Jesus, gathered with their Master for what would become a profoundly transformative evening.

It began with a somber tone as Jesus sat with them for the Passover meal, a tradition steeped in the Jewish heritage. Little did they fully grasp the gravity of what was unfolding. As they reclined at the table, sharing in the bread and wine, Jesus dropped a bombshell that cut through the air like a knife: *"Truly I tell you, one of you will betray me"* (Matthew 26:21, NIV).

Could you imagine the shock and disbelief that rippled through their small circle. Each of them looked around, questioning their own hearts, wondering if they could be the one to commit such a betrayal. Jesus knew their thoughts and continued to share the weight of this revelation: *"The Son of Man will go just as it is written about him. But woe to that man who betrays the Son of Man! It would be better for him if he had not been born"* (Matthew 26:24, NIV).

Judas, sitting among them, then dared to ask, *"Surely you don't mean me, Rabbi?"* And Jesus confirmed, *"You have said so"* (Matthew 26:25, NIV). The reality of his impending betrayal hung heavy in the room as Jesus, with a heart undoubtedly heavy with sorrow, continued to minister to them.

Amidst these intense moments, Jesus took the opportunity to institute a new covenant with them through the breaking of bread and sharing of the cup. He spoke words that would echo through the ages, transforming the traditional Passover meal into a profound symbol of His impending sacrifice: *"This is my body given for you; do this in remembrance of me"* (Luke 22:19, NIV).

Yet, even as they struggled to comprehend the depth of Jesus' words, the shadow of betrayal loomed large. Jesus disclosed, *"But the hand of him who is going to betray me is with mine on the table"* (Luke 22:21, NIV). The weight of these revelations seemed almost unbearable as they struggle with the reality of what lay ahead.

THE CRUCIFIXION

Amidst their confusion and questions, a contentious discussion arose among them about greatness and who among them would be the greatest in the kingdom of heaven. Jesus, always the embodiment of humility and wisdom, gently corrected their misguided ambitions: "*But not so with you. Instead, the greatest among you should be like the youngest, and the one who rules like the one who serves*" (Luke 22:26, NIV).

In these intimate moments, Jesus reminded them that true greatness is found in serving others selflessly, echoing His own example of servant leadership. He assured them of their roles in His kingdom and the importance of unity and humility among His followers.

However, amidst these profound teachings, Jesus turned His gaze to Simon and delivered a sobering prophecy: "*Simon, Simon, Satan has asked to sift all of you as wheat. But I have prayed for you, Simon, that your faith may not fail. And when you have turned back, strengthen your brothers*" (Luke 22:31-32, NIV).

Could you imagine the feeling in Simon Peter's heart as Jesus predicted his denial of Him, not once, but three times before the rooster crowed. In Simon Peter's fervor and bravado, he protested, "*Lord, I am ready to go with you to prison and to death*" (Luke 22:33, NIV). Little did he know the weakness of his own resolve and the imminent trial that awaited him.

As the evening wore on, Jesus spoke enigmatically about preparing for the trials that would soon face his disciples. He cryptically mentioned the necessity of swords, which left them puzzled and questioning the practicality of His words in the midst of such spiritual discourse (Luke 22:35-38).

In the midst of these intense and emotional exchanges, Jesus washed his disciple's feet, demonstrating the humility and sacrificial love that characterized His ministry. He modeled servant leadership, teaching them that true greatness lies in serving others with compassion and humility (John 13:1-17).

Throughout that night, Jesus imparted His final teachings and words of comfort to his disciples, preparing them for the unimaginable events that would soon unfold. He prayed for them fervently, entrusting them into the hands of the Father as He faced the impending agony of the cross.

22:00 hours or 10:00 pm

As the night descended deeper into the early hours of Wednesday, Nisan 13, the weight of what lay ahead began to press heavily upon the disciples. Jesus had just shared His final words and teachings with them during the Passover meal, and now they made their way to the Garden of Gethsemane. The air was thick with tension and a sense of foreboding.

The disciples entered the garden, a place of quiet retreat where Jesus often went to pray, accompanied by Peter, James, and John. Jesus, visibly distressed, told them, "*My soul is overwhelmed with sorrow to the point of death. Stay here and keep watch with me*" (Matthew 26:38, NIV). They couldn't fathom the depth of His anguish, but they remained close, earnestly trying to support Him in His time of need.

Jesus went a little farther into the garden and fell with His face to the ground, praying fervently to His Father: "*My Father, if it is possible, may this cup be taken from me. Yet not as I will, but as you will*" (Matthew 26:39, NIV). His words pierced the disciples hearts with intensity and vulnerability. They could see the struggle within Him as He struggled with the impending sacrifice He was called to make for the salvation of humanity.

Returning to find his disciples sleeping, Jesus urged them to, "*Watch and pray so that you will not fall into temptation. The spirit is willing, but the flesh is weak*" (Matthew 26:41, NIV). He understood their

THE CRUCIFIXION

human frailty, yet in His own distress, He sought solace in communion with His Father, crying out again in earnest prayer.

It was then that the betrayer, Judas Iscariot, arrived in the garden, leading a crowd armed with swords and clubs. Judas approached Jesus and kissed Him, a sign to identify Him to the soldiers. In the confusion and chaos that followed, one of the disciples, in a misguided attempt to defend Jesus, struck the servant of the high priest, cutting off his ear. But Jesus, in His mercy and power, healed the man's ear and rebuked the violence of the moment (Luke 22:47-53; John 18:10-11).

The soldiers, overwhelmed by the presence and authority of Jesus, fell back onto the ground. Jesus, ever calm and collected, willingly surrendered Himself to them, fulfilling the scriptures that foretold His betrayal and arrest (John 18:4-9).

From there, Jesus was taken first to Annas, the father-in-law of Caiaphas the high priest, for questioning (John 18:13-14). Meanwhile, in the courtyard, Peter, desperate to know what would become of his beloved Teacher, denied knowing Jesus three times, just as Jesus had predicted (John 18:15-27).

As Peter stood by the fire, warmed by its flickering light, he heard the rooster crow. In that moment, the weight of his denials crashed down upon him, and he wept bitterly, realizing the depth of his weakness and failure (Luke 22:62).

Jesus, during this time, faced false accusations and condemnation before the Sanhedrin, the Jewish ruling council. They spat on Him, blindfolded Him, and struck Him, mocking Him and demanding that He prove His identity as the Son of God (Matthew 26:57-68).

In these dark hours of Wednesday, Nisan 13, the events unfolded with startling speed and intensity. Jesus endured physical abuse, mockery, and betrayal, all leading up to His trial before Caiaphas and the council. Yet, through it all, He remained steadfast in His mission to fulfill the will of His Father and provide salvation for all humanity.

As I reflect on these harrowing events, I am reminded of Jesus' unwavering love and sacrifice. He willingly endured suffering and humiliation for the sake of each one of us, demonstrating His boundless grace and mercy.

WEDNESDAY, NISAN 13

06:00 am

As the first light of Wednesday, Nisan 13, broke through the darkness, the city of Jerusalem stirred with anticipation and tension. Jesus, who had endured a night of betrayal, arrest, and unjust trials, now found Himself standing before Pontius Pilate, the Roman governor. The religious leaders, driven by envy and fear of Jesus' growing influence, brought Him to Pilate, seeking His condemnation.

The disciples witnessed the scene unfold as Pilate questioned Jesus, seeking to find fault with Him. However, Pilate declared, "*I find no basis for a charge against this man*" (Luke 23:4, NIV). Even Herod, to whom Jesus was sent for further questioning, found no fault in Him and returned Him to Pilate (Luke 23:15). Pilate, sensing Jesus' innocence and caught in the political turmoil, attempted to appease the crowd by offering to release Jesus as a gesture of goodwill during the Passover festival (Luke 23:16).

Meanwhile, the chaos escalated. Judas Iscariot, struggled with remorse for betraying Jesus, sought solace in death and hanged himself (Matthew 27:3-10). The religious leaders, determined to rid themselves of Jesus, incited the crowd to demand the release of Barabbas, a notorious criminal, instead of Jesus (Luke 23:18-19). Pilate, yielding to the pressure, handed Jesus over to be crucified, washing his hands of responsibility but echoing the haunting words, "*I am innocent of this man's blood*" (Matthew 27:24, NIV).

THE CRUCIFIXION

As the soldiers took charge of Jesus, they subjected Him to brutal mockery and humiliation. They dressed Him in a scarlet robe, twisted together a crown of thorns, and placed it on His head, then knelt in mock worship, saying, "*Hail, king of the Jews!*" (Matthew 27:29, NIV). They spat on Him and struck Him repeatedly, driving the thorns deeper into His scalp.

The disciples followed, hearts heavy with grief, as Jesus, weakened by beatings and now bearing His cross, stumbled along the road to Golgotha, the place of the skull, where He would be crucified. Simon of Cyrene was compelled to carry Jesus' cross, a scene that left an indelible mark on everyone watching—this innocent man, burdened with our sins, yet displaying strength and grace amidst such cruelty.

At Golgotha, amidst jeers and taunts, Jesus was nailed to the cross. Soldiers divided His clothes among themselves, casting lots for His seamless robe, fulfilling the scriptures (Matthew 27:35-36). As He hung there, enduring unimaginable pain, Jesus spoke words of forgiveness to His executioners and comfort to a criminal crucified beside Him (Luke 23:34, 43).

Throughout it all, Jesus' words echoed in my mind: "*Father, forgive them, for they do not know what they are doing*" (Luke 23:34, NIV). His compassion and love pierced through the darkness of that day, offering hope and redemption even in the midst of His own suffering.

As the hours passed, the sun's light dimmed, and darkness covered the land from noon until three in the afternoon (Luke 23:44). The earth itself seemed to mourn the agony of its Creator. It was a day of darkness and despair, yet also a day of profound significance—the day when Jesus, the Son of God, willingly laid down His life to fulfill the Father's plan of salvation for all humanity.

In the face of such sacrificial love, I am compelled to ponder the depths of Jesus' suffering and the extent of His love for us. He endured the cross, despising its shame, for the joy set before Him—the joy of reconciling us to God and offering eternal life through His death and resurrection (Hebrews 12:2).

09:00 am – (Third hour)

As the sun climbed higher in the sky on Wednesday, Nisan 13, marking the third hour of the day, the scene at Golgotha remained hauntingly vivid. The disciples stood among the crowd, witnessing the culmination of Jesus' journey to the cross. The soldiers carried out their grim task with chilling efficiency, crucifying Jesus and two others between them.

Mark's Gospel records the stark simplicity of the act: *"It was the third hour when they crucified him"* (Mark 15:25, NIV). John adds further detail, painting a picture of the soldiers dividing Jesus' garments and casting lots for his seamless tunic (John 19:23-24). Even in His agonizing moments, the fulfillment of prophecy unfolded before us, reminding us that every detail of Jesus' suffering was foretold centuries earlier.

Around the disciples, the atmosphere was thick with hostility and mockery. Matthew vividly describes how passersby, including the religious leaders, derided Jesus, hurling insults and challenging Him to prove His divine identity by saving Himself (Matthew 27:39-44). They mocked the one who had healed the sick, raised the dead, and spoken words of truth and love.

Amidst the chaos and scorn, a scene of unexpected grace unfolded. Hanging beside Jesus were two criminals, both condemned to die. One of them, moved by Jesus' silent suffering and the peace that radiated from Him even in agony, rebuked the other criminal and acknowledged Jesus' innocence. *"Jesus, remember me when you come into your kingdom,"* he pleaded (Luke 23:42, NIV).

THE CRUCIFIXION

In response, Jesus spoke words that echoed with divine compassion and mercy: *"Truly I tell you, today you will be with me in paradise"* (Luke 23:43, NIV). In that moment, amidst the pain and darkness of the crucifixion, Jesus extended forgiveness and salvation to a repentant soul, demonstrating His boundless love and the purpose of His sacrificial death.

As the disciples stood there, overwhelmed by the gravity of the scene, another act of profound tenderness unfolded. Jesus, aware of His mother Mary standing nearby, entrusted her care to His beloved disciple John. *"Woman, here is your son,"* he said to Mary, and to John, *"Here is your mother"* (John 19:26-27, NIV). In His final hours, Jesus ensured that His mother would be cared for, revealing His deep concern for those He loved even in the midst of His own suffering.

These moments at the cross revealed the heart of Jesus—compassionate, forgiving, and selfless. His words and actions spoke volumes about the purpose of His mission—to reconcile humanity to God through His death and resurrection. As the hours passed and darkness enveloped the land, the disciples pondered the significance of Jesus' sacrifice and the eternal hope it offered to all who would believe.

12:00 noon – (Sixth hour)

As the sixth hour approached on Wednesday, Nisan 13, a darkness unlike any other descended upon Golgotha, where Jesus hung on the cross. The disciples stood among the crowd, bewildered and fearful, as the sky turned black and an eerie silence settled over us.

Mark's Gospel vividly captures this supernatural phenomenon: *"At noon, darkness came over the whole land until three in the afternoon"* (Mark 15:33, NIV). The darkness was more than a mere absence of light; it was a profound manifestation of the cosmic significance of Jesus' sacrifice. It was as if creation itself recoiled at the magnitude of the events unfolding—God's own Son bearing the weight of humanity's sin.

In those moments of darkness, time seemed suspended. The usual noises of the city faded into an unsettling quiet, broken only by occasional sobs and whispers among the onlookers. For three hours, the disciples stood there, contemplating the gravity of what was happening before our eyes. Some pondered the meaning of this darkness, while others were filled with dread and uncertainty.

As they stood in that somber atmosphere, their thoughts turned to the prophecies that foretold this very moment. Amos had spoken of a day when God would make the sun go down at noon and darken the earth in broad daylight (Amos 8:9). Here, before their eyes, that prophecy was being fulfilled in a way that surpassed all human understanding.

The darkness also mirrored the spiritual reality of Jesus' suffering. As He hung on the cross, bearing the sins of the world, He experienced the profound separation from God that sin brings. It was a darkness that encapsulated the weight of humanity's rebellion and the depth of God's love—a love that compelled Him to send His Son to die for us (John 3:16).

In those hours of darkness, the disciples felt a deep sense of awe and reverence. The world around them seemed to stand still as they contemplated the enormity of Jesus' sacrifice and the price He paid for their redemption. The darkness was a reminder of the seriousness of sin and the lengths to which God went to reconcile us to Himself.

And yet, amidst the darkness, there was also a glimmer of hope. The discples remembered Jesus' words earlier in His ministry, when He declared Himself to be the light of the world (John 8:12). Even in this darkest hour, His light was not extinguished. His sacrificial love shone through, offering forgiveness and salvation to all who would believe.

THE CRUCIFIXION

As the hours passed and the darkness lingered, the disciples clung to the promise that beyond the cross lay the hope of resurrection. The darkness would not have the final word; Easter morning would bring the dawn of a new day and the triumph of life over death. Jesus' sacrifice on the cross was the ultimate act of love, bridging the gap between God and humanity and offering eternal hope to all who trust in him.

This reflection captures the solemnity and significance of the darkness that covered the land during the sixth hour on Wednesday, Nisan 13, emphasizing the spiritual and prophetic dimensions of Jesus' crucifixion.

3:00pm – (Ninth hour)

As the ninth hour approached on Wednesday, Nisan 13, the world around the disciples seemed to hold its breath. The events of the day had been tumultuous, leading to this pivotal moment when everything changed.

At exactly 3:00 pm, a chill ran down the disciples spine as they recalled the eerie darkness that had shrouded Golgotha for three hours. The air was heavy with an inexplicable solemnity, and even the soldiers seemed to sense that something momentous was happening.

Matthew's Gospel recounts the haunting cry that pierced the darkness: "*About three in the afternoon Jesus cried out in a loud voice, 'Eli, Eli, lema sabachthani?' (which means 'My God, my God, why have you forsaken me?')*" (Matthew 27:46, NIV). These words echoed with a depth of anguish that reverberated through the hearts of all who heard them.

In that moment, Jesus experienced the full weight of separation from God. As Paul later wrote, "*God made him who had no sin to be sin for us, so that in him we might become the righteousness of God*" (2 Corinthians 5:21, NIV). Jesus, who knew no sin, willingly took upon Himself the sins of the world. The separation He felt was not just physical but spiritual—a profound agony that fulfilled the deepest depths of prophecy and redemption.

John's Gospel further illuminates the scene: "*Later, knowing that everything had now been finished, and so that Scripture would be fulfilled, Jesus said, 'I am thirsty'*" (John 19:28, NIV). His thirst was not merely physical but symbolic of the completion of His earthly mission. With these words, Jesus signaled that the time had come for the final act of sacrifice and fulfillment.

Then, with a voice that echoed across eternity, Jesus declared, "*It is finished*" (John 19:30, NIV). In these three words, He proclaimed the culmination of God's plan of salvation. The veil in the temple tore from top to bottom, symbolizing the opening of the way to God for all who would believe (Matthew 27:51). The earthquake that followed underscored the cosmic significance of what had just occurred—the earth itself responding to the sacrifice of the Son of God.

In the midst of this turmoil, the confession of the centurion pierced the air: "*Surely He was the Son of God!*" (Matthew 27:54, NIV). Even a hardened Roman soldier recognized the divine nature of Jesus' sacrifice and the truth of his identity.

As the disciples stood among the crowd, witnessing these events unfold, a profound conviction settled in their hearts. Luke's Gospel captures it well: "*When all the people who had gathered to witness this sight saw what took place, they beat their breasts and went away*" (Luke 23:48, NIV). The people were deeply moved by what they had seen and heard, recognizing the gravity of their own sin and the magnitude of God's love displayed on the cross.

John's Gospel continues with the detail of the soldiers breaking the legs of the criminals crucified with Jesus, but finding Him already dead, they pierced His side with a spear (John 19:31-37). Blood and water

THE CRUCIFIXION

flowed, symbolizing the cleansing and life-giving power of Jesus' sacrifice—a sacrifice that fulfilled the Passover lamb's ultimate purpose.

In these moments at 3:00 pm on that Wednesday, Nisan 13, the world was forever changed. Jesus had completed His mission, fulfilling every prophecy and offering salvation to all who would believe.

THURSDAY NISAN 14

18:00 hours or 6:00 pm (End of Wednesday – beginning of Thursday)

As the sun dipped low on the horizon, casting long shadows across Jerusalem, the disciple's hearts were heavy with the events of the day. The air was thick with tension and sorrow as they hurriedly prepared to lay Jesus to rest before the Sabbath began. The events had unfolded swiftly, like a torrential storm that had swept through their lives, leaving them bewildered and deeply shaken.

Earlier in the day, as the evening approached, a sense of urgency gripped the disciples. Jesus' lifeless body lay in the tomb, a somber reminder of the cruelty and injustice He endured. They were determined to honour Him in His death, despite the risks and the overwhelming grief that threatened to engulf them.

According to John's account, Joseph of Arimathea, a respected member of the council, came forward courageously. He boldly asked Pilate for permission to take Jesus' body down from the cross. Alongside him was Nicodemus, who brought a mixture of myrrh and aloes, about seventy-five pounds in weight, to anoint Jesus' body for burial.

I could sense the weight of their sorrow as they carefully removed Jesus' body from the cross. Every movement seemed to echo the finality of His death. They wrapped His body in linen cloths with the spices, according to the burial customs of the Jews. This was no ordinary burial;

it was an act of profound love and reverence for the Teacher who had touched so many lives.

As they laid Jesus in the tomb, hewn out of rock, the disciples hearts ached with a mixture of disbelief and deep sorrow. The stone slab was rolled into place, sealing Him within. Yet, even in the midst of their despair, a glimmer of hope flickered faintly. The disciples remembered His words about rising again on the third day.

Meanwhile, the religious leaders, fearful of Jesus' prediction that He would rise from the dead, approached Pilate. They reminded him of Jesus' claim that He would rise after three days and nights.

As the disciples sat in the silence of the Sabbath morning, their minds wandered to Jesus' words about rising again after three days. It seemed impossible, surreal even, yet His assurance lingered in their hearts like a whisper of hope amidst the despair. Little did they know that while they mourned His death, something miraculous was unfolding beyond their comprehension.

Scripture tells us that during this time, Jesus descended into Hades. It wasn't a descent of defeat or punishment, but rather a triumph over the powers of darkness. In Hades, He proclaimed victory to the spirits who were held captive, fulfilling a purpose that transcended our earthly understanding.

The Apostle Peter later wrote about this in his epistle, mentioning how Jesus preached to the spirits in prison who were disobedient in the days of Noah. This wasn't about condemnation but about redemption, offering even those who had perished before His time on earth a chance to hear the message of salvation.

As I pondered these mysteries, I couldn't help but marvel at the depth of Jesus' love and the breadth of His mission. Even in His death, He was actively working to reconcile all things to Himself, bridging the gap between God and humanity in a way that only He could.

THE CRUCIFIXION

The Passover Sabbath continued, its usual rhythms juxtaposed against the extraordinary events unfolding in the spiritual realm. While the disciples observed the traditions of their faith, unaware of the profound implications of Jesus' sacrifice, He was fulfilling the ultimate Passover Lamb role—delivering us from the bondage of sin and death.

In the midst of the disciple's sorrow and confusion, there was a glimmer of hope—a hope that transcended the darkness of the tomb and the depths of Hades. Jesus' journey didn't end on the cross; it was a prelude to the greatest victory the world would ever know.

FRIDAY NISAN 15

18:00 hours or 6:00 pm – (End of Thursday – beginning of Friday)

As the sun set, signaling the end of Thursday and the start of Friday, Nisan 15, the disciples were feeling still reeling from the events of the past days. The city was quieter than usual, a solemn hush hanging over Jerusalem as the Feast of Unleavened Bread Sabbath began. For many, it was a day of rest and religious observance, but for the disciples who had followed Jesus, it was a day marked by a peculiar tension—a mixture of sorrow, anticipation, and lingering uncertainty.

As the disciples reflected on the previous day, the image of Jesus on the cross haunted their thoughts. The brutality of His crucifixion, the anguish in His voice, and the weight of His sacrifice weighed heavily on their hearts. They had witnessed the Son of God, the promised Messiah, bearing the sins of the world. The darkness that had covered the land during His final moments had mirrored the darkness in their souls.

Yet, amid the despair, there was a thread of hope—a hope rooted in Jesus' own words about rising again after three days. It was a promise that seemed impossible and yet carried a glimmer of light in the midst of the disciples' grief.

As I contemplated these events, I marveled at the depth of Jesus' love and the breadth of His mission. Even in His death, He was actively working to reconcile all things to Himself, bridging the gap between God and humanity in a way that only He could.

The Feast of Unleavened Bread Sabbath continued, its rituals and observances unfolding as they had for generations. Yet, unbeknownst to many, including the disciples, something extraordinary was happening beyond their understanding. While they honoured the traditions of their faith, Jesus was fulfilling the ultimate role of the Passover Lamb—delivering them from the bondage of sin and death, not just for a year but for all eternity.

In the silence of that Sabbath day, the disciples found themselves wrestling with conflicting emotions—grief over the loss of their Teacher, uncertainty about what the future held, and a flicker of hope that burned brighter with each passing hour. Jesus' journey didn't end on the cross; it was a prelude to the greatest victory the world would ever know.

As the day drew to a close and the sun dipped below the horizon, I couldn't help but wonder what tomorrow, the Sabbath, would bring. Little did I know that dawn would reveal an empty tomb, shattered chains of death, and a risen Saviour who had conquered sin, defeated death, and brought forth new life for all who would believe.

SATURDAY NISAN 16

18:00 hours or 6:00 pm – (End of Friday – beginning of Saturday)

As the sun set below the horizon, signaling the end of Friday and the start of Saturday, Nisan 16, the disciples were feeling a strange mix of anticipation and uncertainty. The previous day, they had observed the Feast of Unleavened Bread Sabbath, a solemn time marked by the events surrounding Jesus' crucifixion and His descent into Hades. Now,

THE CRUCIFIXION

it was the weekly Sabbath—the day of rest and reflection ingrained in the Jewish tradition.

The city of Jerusalem seemed quieter than usual, still carrying the weight of recent events. Many were observing the Sabbath in their homes or at the synagogue, but for the disciples who had followed Jesus, it was a day overshadowed by questions and a sense of waiting. They had seen their Teacher and Lord crucified, witnessed the earth shaking and the sky darkening, and heard of His descent into the realm of the dead.

In the silence of that Saturday, the disciples wrestled with the mystery of Jesus' descent into Hades. It wasn't a defeat or a punishment but a victorious proclamation of His triumph over sin and death. The words of Scripture echoed in their minds, reminding them of God's plan of redemption unfolding through Christ's sacrificial death and resurrection.

The weekly Sabbath continued, its rituals and observances proceeding as they had for generations. Yet, for the other disciples, this Sabbath held a deeper significance. It was a time of waiting—waiting for the fulfillment of Jesus' promise to rise again on the third day.

Throughout the day, the disciples found solace in prayer and reflection, seeking understanding and peace in the midst of uncertainty. The words of the prophets and Psalms came to mind, offering comfort and assurance that God's purposes would not be thwarted.

As the sun began to set and the Sabbath drew to a close, the disciple's hearts were filled with a mixture of hope and apprehension. The next day would mark the third day since Jesus' crucifixion—the day we had been anticipating with both fear and longing. Little did they know that dawn would reveal an empty tomb, shattered chains of death, and a risen Saviour who had conquered sin and opened the way to eternal life for all who would believe.

SUNDAY NISAN 17

18:00 hours or 6:00 pm – (End of Saturday – beginning of Sunday)

RESURRECTION

As the sun dipped below the horizon, signaling the end of Saturday and the start of Sunday, Nisan 17, the air was heavy with a mix of anticipation and uncertainty among the disciples. They had witnessed the unimaginable—their beloved Teacher, Jesus, crucified and laid to rest in a borrowed tomb. The events of the past days had left us reeling, questioning the future and struggling with grief. Little did we know that this evening would mark the most profound turning point in human history.

Acts 13:33 echoed in the disciple's mind,s a reminder that Jesus, through His resurrection, was justified and raised to life by God's power. It was a moment of divine vindication, where God's plan for salvation reached its climax.

Reflecting on the Scriptures (1 Timothy 3:16; 1 Peter 3:18; Ephesians 2:5-6), I marveled at how God accomplished this miraculous resurrection. It was through His powerful word (Hebrews 1:5-13), spoken into the darkness of death, that Jesus emerged victorious. Colossians 2:15 assured me that Jesus not only conquered death but also disarmed the spiritual forces of evil, stripping them of their power.

The resurrection was not merely a physical event; it was a cosmic victory. Hebrews 2:14 reminded me that through His death and resurrection, Jesus rendered powerless the devil, who held humanity in bondage through fear of death. 1 John 3:8 resonated deeply—the Son of God appeared to destroy the works of the devil, and His resurrection sealed that victory.

At dawn, as the women made their way to the tomb, they encountered an earthquake (Matthew 28:1-8) and found the tomb

THE CRUCIFIXION

empty. The stone rolled away, the guards stunned into silence, and the angel's proclamation confirmed what Jesus had foretold—He had risen from the dead!

Mary Magdalene's encounter with the risen Lord (John 20:11-17) was a moment of profound joy and awe. Jesus, whom we had seen crucified and buried, stood before her alive! His words to her, "*Do not cling to me, for I have not yet ascended to the Father,*" (John 20:17) revealed the significance of His resurrection and the dawn of a new era.

In Galilee, as Jesus appeared to His disciples, His presence confirmed His victory over death. His commission in Matthew 28:16-20 was clear—to go and make disciples of all nations, baptizing them in the name of the Father, Son, and Holy Spirit. With hearts full of wonder and determination, they received His charge and witnessed His ascension into heaven.

Every appearance of Jesus affirmed His resurrection and His victory. From Peter (Luke 24:34; 1 Corinthians 15:5), who saw Him first among the disciples, to the two disciples on the road to Emmaus (Luke 24:13-35), the eleven gathered in Jerusalem (Luke 24:36-43), and the 500 others (1 Corinthians 15:6) who witnessed His resurrected form, His presence was tangible proof of His triumph over death. Even doubting Thomas (John 20:24-29) was convinced when he touched the scars on Jesus' hands and side.

The account in John 21:1-24, where Jesus appeared to his disciples while they were fishing in Galilee, solidified their faith. His presence and the miraculous catch of fish were signs of His resurrection and His continued care for His followers.

Reflecting on these profound events and encounters, I am filled with gratitude and awe. The resurrection of Jesus Christ is the foundation of our faith, the ultimate demonstration of God's love and power. Through His resurrection, we have hope of eternal life, forgiveness of sins, and a restored relationship with God. His victory over death brings freedom and new life to all who believe in Him.

THE CRUCIFIXION

THE CROSS

As I reflect on the profound question of what the blood did for us on the cross, I'm drawn into a journey of deep significance and eternal importance. It's not just a theological concept or a distant historical event; rather, it's a reality that has the power to transform lives and shape destinies for all eternity. The blood shed on the cross holds the key to our salvation, our redemption, and our reconciliation with God.

For me, this question evokes memories of my own journey of faith and the moments when I first began to grasp the profound meaning of Jesus' sacrifice on the cross. Like many, I grew into hearing about the crucifixion of Jesus, but it wasn't until later I explore the scriptures that I truly began to understand the significance of His shed blood. It was through moments of personal reflection, study, and prayer that I began to grasp the depth of God's love revealed through the sacrifice of His Son. There were times when all I could do is thank the Lord for dying for me. And with a heartfelt love, tears would stream down my cheeks, and I am embraced by the presence of the Holy Spirit.

As I explore this question, I'm reminded of the words of the apostle Paul, who eloquently captured the essence of what the blood did for us

THE CROSS

on the cross in his letter to the Ephesians. He wrote, "*In him we have redemption through his blood, the forgiveness of sins, in accordance with the riches of God's grace*" (Ephesians 1:7, NIV). These words speak to the heart of the gospel message and encapsulate the transformative power of Jesus' sacrifice.

As I ponder the profound words penned by Paul in his letter to the Colossians, I'm struck by the depth of the spiritual realities he unveils. He speaks of events that transcend the physical realm, occurrences that took place beyond our ordinary understanding of time and space.

In Christ, Paul tells us, the fullness of God was pleased to dwell, and through Him, all things were reconciled to God, both on earth and in heaven. This reconciliation, Paul emphasizes, was accomplished through the blood of Christ's cross.

The imagery Paul paints is powerful and evocative. He describes Jesus' death on the cross as a spiritual battle, a clash between the forces of good and evil, between the powers of heaven and hell.

Through His sacrificial death, Jesus confronted and disarmed every evil force, triumphing over them completely. In doing so, He made peace by His blood, reconciling humanity to God and breaking the power of sin and death.

What's remarkable is that this victory wasn't just for humanity's sake. It was a victory that reverberated throughout the entire universe, impacting even the heavenly realms. Jesus' death on the cross had spiritual implications, bringing about a restoration of all things and ushering in a new era of reconciliation and redemption. No longer would humanity be estranged and hostile toward God; through Christ's death, we are made holy, blameless, and irreproachable before Him.

In the letter to the Hebrews, this victory is further underscored. Jesus, in taking on human flesh and blood, entered into our world to confront the very source of our bondage: the devil and the fear of death.

Through Jesus' death, He destroyed the power of death and liberated all those who were held captive by the fear of its grip. It's a profound truth that speaks to the heart of our faith: in Christ, we find freedom from the tyranny of sin and death, and in His blood, we find the assurance of our redemption and reconciliation with God.

As I reflect on these passages, I'm reminded of the immense love and sacrifice displayed by Jesus on the cross. His death wasn't just a historical event; it was a spiritual victory that echoes throughout eternity. It's a victory that I, as a believer, am privileged to share in, knowing that through His blood, I am made whole, reconciled to God, and set free from the power of sin and death.

It's a staggering thought to imagine Jesus facing the full onslaught of demonic forces, fallen angels, and the power of evil in the heavenly realms as He hung on the cross. Yet, in His sacrificial act, Jesus disarmed them completely, triumphing over them and reconciling all things to God.

Through death, Jesus brought about peace, bridging the divide between God and humanity, and offering reconciliation to all who would believe.

The victory Jesus achieved on the cross extends far beyond the confines of earthly existence. In the letter to the Hebrews, we're reminded of the profound significance of Jesus' death in overcoming humanity's greatest enemy: death itself. Jesus, by taking on human flesh and blood, entered into our world to confront the very source of our bondage—the devil and the fear of death. Through His death, He shattered the power of death and liberated all who were held captive by its grip.

It is for the final outworking in history of Satan's defeat at the cross that we now eagerly await. What is the completed work of Christ on the cross in the eternal time frame will come to pass in human history at God's appointed time on our earthly calendars.

As I reflect on the significance of Christ's victory on the cross, I'm reminded that it's not just a past event but a reality that continues to shape the course of history. The defeat of Satan at the cross marked a pivotal moment in the eternal realm, but its full manifestation in human history is yet to come. We eagerly await the final outworking of this victory, knowing that what Christ accomplished on the cross will ultimately be realized in God's perfect timing.

In the eternal time frame, the defeat of Satan and the triumph of Christ are already secured. Through His death and resurrection, Jesus dealt a decisive blow to the powers of darkness, ensuring their ultimate defeat. The cross was not just a temporary setback for Satan; it was the beginning of his downfall.

As believers, we take comfort in knowing that the battle has been won, even if we have yet to see its complete fulfillment in our earthly lives.

However, while we wait for the final realization of Christ's victory, we must also recognize that it has profound implications for our lives here and now. The power of the cross is not limited to the future; it has immediate significance for our present reality. Through faith in Christ, we can experience freedom from sin, restoration to God, and victory over the forces of evil in our lives. The cross is not just a historical event; it's a living reality that continues to transform hearts and lives today.

As we eagerly await the final consummation of Christ's victory, we must live in anticipation of God's ultimate triumph over evil. We do not lose heart in the face of trials and tribulations, knowing that the victory has already been won. Instead, we cling to the hope that one day, Christ's victory will be fully revealed, and every knee will bow and every tongue confess that Jesus Christ is Lord. Until then, we live as witnesses to the power of the cross, proclaiming the good news of salvation and eagerly anticipating the day when Christ's victory will be fully realized in human history.

As I ponder the events leading up to Jesus' crucifixion, I can't help but be struck by the profound truth that Jesus became sin for us. It's a concept that's both awe-inspiring and deeply humbling. In Matthew 27:45, we see Jesus hanging on the cross, bearing the weight of the sins of the world. He willingly took upon Himself the guilt and shame of every wrongdoing, past, present, and future. It's a sacrifice beyond comprehension, a love beyond measure.

In verse 46, we glimpse the full extent of Jesus' suffering as He cries out, "My God, my God, why have you forsaken me?" In that moment, Jesus experienced the ultimate separation from God, as the weight of humanity's sin fell upon Him. It's a moment of profound anguish, as the Son of God, who had known perfect communion with the Father for all eternity, feels the pain of abandonment.

Yet, even in His darkest hour, Jesus remained obedient to the Father's will, bearing our sins until the very end.

"For He made Him who knew no sin to be sin for us, that we might become the righteousness of God in Him." **2 Corinthians 5:21**

This verse encapsulates the heart of the gospel message – that Jesus, the sinless Son of God, willingly took our place on the cross, bearing the punishment we deserved, so that we might be reconciled to God. It's a divine exchange – our sin for His righteousness – made possible through the sacrificial death of Jesus Christ.

The word "made" in this verse carries significant weight. It wasn't merely a symbolic act or a superficial gesture. Jesus wasn't just offering a sin offering; He was actually becoming sin itself. He took on our sinfulness in its entirety, so that we might be clothed in His righteousness. It's a profound mystery, the depth of which we can

THE CROSS

scarcely comprehend. But it's a truth that changes everything – our past, our present, and our future.

As I reflect on Jesus' willingness to become sin for me, I'm overwhelmed by the magnitude of His love. It's a love that knows no bounds, that surpasses all understanding. It's a love that took Him to the cross, that endured the agony of separation from the Father, all for the sake of my salvation. It's a love that calls me to respond with gratitude, humility, and devotion. May I never forget the price that was paid for my redemption, and may I live each day in the light of His sacrificial love.

As I continue to delve into the depths of Scripture, I'm struck by the profound truth that over 80 translations state that God made Jesus to sin. It's a concept that challenges our understanding and stretches our faith, but it's at the very heart of the gospel message. One translation, the Jerusalem Bible, puts it succinctly: "God made the sinless one into sin." This truth reveals the incredible depth of God's love for us – that He would go to such lengths to reconcile us to Himself.

God made Jesus to be sin so that we might become the righteousness of God in Him. It's a divine exchange, as Jesus takes upon Himself our sinfulness and in return, offers us His righteousness. It's a transaction beyond comprehension, a grace beyond measure. In the eyes of God, we are redeemed, forgiven, and set free from the power of sin and death.

It's at the cross that the greatest transaction in human history takes place, as Jesus takes upon Himself the weight of our sins and offers us His perfect righteousness. It's a transaction that transforms us from the inside out, as we are made new in Christ Jesus.

Sin, we must remember, is not just an action; it's a nature – a nature that separates us from God and enslaves us to our own desires. But Jesus, in His infinite love and mercy, came to earth, taking on human flesh, so that we might become like Him. He experienced every temptation, every trial, every hardship, yet remained without sin. In Him, we find the perfect example of what it means to live a life fully surrendered to God.

As I contemplate the magnitude of God's love revealed at the cross, I'm reminded that I am no longer bound by the chains of sin and death. Through Jesus' sacrifice, I have been set free to live a life of righteousness.

When I reflect on the words penned by Peter in his first epistle, I'm struck by the profound truth they convey about the sacrifice of Jesus. He bore our sins in His own body on the tree – the cross – so that we, being dead to sins, might live unto righteousness. And not only that, but by His stripes, we were healed. It's a message of redemption and healing, woven together in the fabric of God's grace.

As I meditate on these words, I can't help but marvel at the selflessness of Jesus' act. He took upon Himself the weight of our sins, carrying them to the cross, so that we wouldn't have to bear them ourselves. It's a love beyond comprehension – that He would endure such agony and suffering on our behalf, simply out of love for us.

Jesus did it all so that we don't have to do it. He carried the burden of sin and shame so that we could walk in freedom and righteousness. He bore the pain and the stripes so that we could experience healing and wholeness. It's a gift of grace, freely given, but one that cost Him everything.

I'm reminded of a simple analogy: if someone were to help me carry a heavy load to my car, only for me to take it back and carry it myself, wouldn't they be offended? In the same way, Jesus bore our sins and our burdens so that we could be free, so that we could live in the fullness of His grace.

Let us never forget the price that was paid for our redemption and let us live each day in gratitude for the love that was demonstrated on the cross.

In Leviticus, I come across a peculiar ritual known as the scapegoat ceremony. It's a symbolic act where one goat is sent out into the wilderness, carrying away the sins of the people and into Satan's territory. Anyone who touches it becomes unclean. It's a vivid illustration of the transfer of guilt and the removal of sin from the community.

Interestingly, I stumble upon John the Baptist's proclamation in the Gospel of John, where he points to Jesus as the Lamb of God who takes away the sins of the world. Suddenly, the pieces start to come together. John wasn't just speaking metaphorically; he was alluding to the scapegoat of Leviticus, the one who would bear the sins of humanity and carry them away.

Jesus Himself confirms this imagery when He likens His impending crucifixion to Moses lifting the serpent in the wilderness. It's a profound statement that speaks to the nature of His sacrifice – not just a physical death, but a symbolic act of taking on the sins of the world.

In 2 Corinthians 5:21, Paul elucidates the purpose behind Jesus becoming sin for us. It wasn't merely for dramatic effect; it was so that we could become righteous. This echoes the prophetic words of Isaiah in chapter 53, where he vividly describes the suffering and sacrifice of the Messiah.

Isaiah paints a picture of Jesus bearing our sins upon Himself, enduring the judgment and sentence that rightfully belonged to us. It's a sobering realization – that He willingly went to the cross, facing a sudden and agonizing death for the transgressions of humanity.

Yet amidst the darkness, there is a glimmer of hope. Isaiah declares that it pleased the Lord to bruise Him, not out of sadistic pleasure, but because through His suffering, we can be redeemed. God made Him an offering for our sins, and in His sacrifice, justice is satisfied.

As I ponder these profound truths, I'm struck by the depth of God's love and the magnitude of Jesus' sacrifice. He willingly took upon Himself the weight of our sins, enduring unimaginable agony so that we could be made righteous. It's a sacrifice beyond comprehension, but one that I am eternally grateful for.

I stumble upon a profound revelation regarding the concept of death. In Hebrew, the word "death" is plural, signifying not just the cessation of physical life but also a spiritual separation from God. It's a concept that goes beyond mere mortality and into the very essence of our existence.

What strikes me is the realization that while the Gospel writers Matthew, Mark, Luke, and John chronicled Jesus' life and ministry, they didn't witness the moment when Jesus bore the weight of sin upon Himself. Yet, as I explore the Psalms, particularly Psalm 22, I find myself transported to the very scene of Jesus' crucifixion.

As Jesus hung upon the cross, His agonizing cry, "My God, my God, why have you forsaken me?" echoes the words penned by David centuries earlier. It's as though David, in his prophetic insight, was present at the foot of the cross, bearing witness to the unfolding events.

In Psalm 22, David vividly describes the depths of Jesus' anguish – the weight of sin bearing down upon Him, the agonizing separation from the holiness of God, and yet, amidst the darkness, the unwavering trust in God's promises of resurrection.

What strikes me most is the poignant imagery of Jesus as a worm, spiritually dead, so that we might be made righteous. It's a sobering reminder of the extent of His sacrifice and the depth of His love for humanity.

As I read further, I'm struck by the vivid descriptions of Jesus' suffering – His heart ruptured, His bones out of joint, and the blood and water flowing from His side. It's a scene that mirrors the reality of crucifixion, yet it's also a fulfillment of prophecy, a testament to the divine plan unfolding before our eyes.

And as I reflect on David's words, penned centuries before Jesus' birth, I'm reminded of God's plan – how every detail, every prophecy, points to the ultimate sacrifice of Jesus on the cross. It's a reminder that even in the darkest moments, God's hand is at work, orchestrating redemption and restoration for all humanity.

As I ponder over the profound truth encapsulated in Galatians 3:13-14, I am struck by the gravity of what it means for Jesus to become a curse for us. It's a concept that challenges the very essence of our understanding of redemption and sacrifice.

"Christ redeemed us from the curse of the law by becoming a curse for us, for it is written: "Cursed is everyone who is hung on a pole." He redeemed us in order that the blessing given to Abraham might come to the Gentiles through Christ Jesus, so that by faith we might receive the promise of the Spirit." **Galatians 3:13-14**

Imagine, if you will, the weight of every curse, every consequence of sin, laid upon the shoulders of Jesus as He hung upon the cross. It's a burden too heavy for any mortal to bear, yet Jesus, in His infinite love and mercy, willingly took it upon Himself.

In that moment, Jesus bore not just the physical pain of crucifixion but the spiritual weight of every curse that had separated humanity from God. It's a sacrifice that defies comprehension – the sinless Son of God willingly becoming a curse so that we might be set free.

As I explore deeper into the passage, I'm struck by the significance of Jesus' act of redemption. Through His death on the cross, He not only bore the curse of the law but also broke its power over us. It's a victory that reverberates throughout eternity, offering hope and freedom to all who believe.

And yet, amidst the darkness of sin and death, there shines a glimmer of hope – the promise of redemption and restoration. Through Jesus' sacrificial death, we are not only freed from the curse of the law but also empowered to live in righteousness and holiness.

As I reflect on these truths, I am reminded of the immense love that Jesus has for each and every one of us. He willingly endured the shame and agony of the cross so that we might experience the fullness of God's grace and mercy.

In Deuteronomy 28, I am confronted with the stark reality of the curse of the law. The chapter begins with a list of blessings – promises of prosperity, abundance, and divine favour for those who obey the commandments of God. But as I continue reading, I am met with a much longer list of curses – consequences for disobedience, ranging from sickness and poverty to ultimate destruction.

It's a sobering realization that the same law that promises blessings also carries the weight of curses for those who fail to uphold it. And yet, amidst the detailed descriptions of suffering and hardship, there is a glimmer of hope – a promise of redemption and restoration.

As I ponder over verses 15 to 68, I am struck by the depth of suffering that is described. Poverty, sickness, and sin are depicted as the inevitable result of disobedience to God's commands. It's a grim picture of the consequences of rebellion against the divine will.

And yet, in the midst of this darkness, there is a ray of hope. For it is in these very curses that Jesus found Himself on the cross. Every sickness, every affliction, every curse that was pronounced in Deuteronomy 28, Jesus bore upon Himself as He hung on Calvary's hill.

Verse 15 reminds us that it is not God who curses us, but rather the natural consequences of our disobedience. Yet even in allowing these curses to come upon us, God's ultimate purpose is redemption. He desires for us to turn back to Him, to repent of our sins, and to experience His grace and mercy.

And so, as I reflect on Deuteronomy 28, I am reminded of the profound truth that Jesus became the embodiment of these curses so that we might be set free. He endured the full weight of our sin and suffering so that we might experience the blessings of redemption and restoration.

Jesus Christ, who became a curse for us so that we might be redeemed from the curse of the law. It's a message of hope and salvation for all who turn to Him in faith.

As I ponder over Galatians 3:13, I am struck by the profound truth it holds – that we have been redeemed from every disease, sickness, and curse. It's a statement that carries immense weight and significance, offering hope and healing to those who are suffering.

The concept of redemption is one that resonates deeply with me. It's a word that speaks of liberation, of being set free from bondage and captivity. And in the context of Galatians 3:13, it speaks of Jesus Christ's ultimate act of redemption on the cross.

When I think about the word "redeemed," I can't help but picture a scene of a marketplace, where a transaction is taking place. In this transaction, Jesus is the buyer, and we are the ones being bought back – purchased with His own precious blood. It's a powerful image that speaks to the costliness of our redemption.

But what exactly does it mean to be redeemed from every disease, sickness, and curse? It means that Jesus bore upon Himself every affliction known to mankind – from the common cold to the most debilitating illness. It means that His sacrifice on the cross was sufficient to wash away every sin, every sickness, and every curse that humanity could ever face.

As I meditate on this truth, I am filled with awe and gratitude for the magnitude of Jesus' sacrifice. He didn't just die for our sins – He died to bring healing and wholeness to every area of our lives. His blood has the power to cleanse us from all unrighteousness, to heal our bodies, and to set us free from the bondage of sin and sickness.

And so, as I reflect on Galatians 3:13, I am reminded of the incredible love and compassion of our Saviour. He willingly took upon Himself the weight of our sins and our sufferings so that we might experience freedom and abundant life. It's a truth that fills me with hope and confidence, knowing that I am redeemed by the precious blood of Jesus Christ.

Isaiah 52:13 unveils a profound revelation that continues to resonate with me deeply. It's a passage that speaks to the astonishing nature of Jesus Christ's sacrifice on the cross, a sacrifice that transcends human comprehension.

As I reflect on Isaiah's words, I can't help but imagine the scene he describes – the people's astonishment at Jesus, their disbelief at the sight before them. They beheld a figure so marred and disfigured that He hardly resembled a human being. It's a haunting image that speaks to the immense suffering and humiliation that Jesus endured on our behalf.

The imagery painted by Isaiah's prophecy is vivid and powerful, underscoring the depth of Jesus' sacrifice. The Hebrews described Him as so disfigured that He appeared like a mere piece of flesh, a shocking portrayal of the extent to which He bore the weight of our sins and curses. Even the Living Bible emphasizes the severity of His appearance, highlighting the profound transformation He underwent for our redemption.

THE CROSS

In becoming a curse for us, Jesus took upon Himself the full weight of our transgressions, our sicknesses, and our afflictions. He willingly entered into our brokenness and suffering, bearing it all so that we might be set free. It's a truth that speaks to the boundless love and mercy of our Saviour, who spared no expense to secure our redemption.

To truly grasp the magnitude of Jesus' sacrifice, we must turn to the Spirit of revelation and allow the prophets to illuminate the full picture for us. It's through their insights and revelations that we gain a deeper understanding of the profound mysteries of God's plan of salvation. And as we look into the depths of Scripture, we come to realize the immeasurable value of Jesus' sacrifice and the boundless grace He extends to each one of us.

Sometimes I find myself pondering the question: Why did Jesus become a curse? It's a thought that lingers in the back of my mind, prompting me to search deeper into the Scriptures in search of answers. And as I explore passages like 2 Corinthians 3:14, I begin to unravel the profound significance of Jesus' sacrificial act.

One of the reasons why Jesus took on the curse was so that we could inherit the blessings promised to Abraham. You see, in Deuteronomy 28:1-14, God outlines a series of blessings that He promised to bestow upon His people if they remained obedient to His commands. These blessings encompassed every aspect of life – from prosperity and success to protection and favour. And through His death on the cross, Jesus made it possible for us to partake in these blessings, regardless of our own shortcomings or failures.

It's a truth that fills me with awe and gratitude, knowing that in Christ, I have access to the same blessings that were promised to Abraham centuries ago. It's a testament to the richness of God's grace and the depth of His love for each one of us. And as I reflect on this reality, I'm reminded of the immeasurable value of Jesus' sacrifice and the boundless blessings that await those who put their trust in Him.

JESUS: MY ROLE MODEL

But that's not all. Another reason why Jesus became a curse was so that we could receive the Holy Spirit. You see, through His death and resurrection, Jesus opened the way for the Holy Spirit to dwell within us, empowering us to live lives that are pleasing to God. It's through the Holy Spirit that we are transformed from the inside out, renewed in our minds and hearts, and equipped to walk in obedience to God's will.

As I contemplate the significance of Jesus' sacrifice and the blessings it has bestowed upon me, I'm filled with a deep sense of gratitude and reverence. It's a reminder of the incredible privilege we have as believers – to be heirs of God's promises and vessels of His Spirit. And it's a call to live lives that reflect the love, grace, and power of our Saviour, who willingly became a curse so that we might experience the fullness of God's blessings and the presence of His Spirit in our lives.

You know, there's a passage in Isaiah 53 that always strikes a chord with me – Isaiah paints this vivid picture of Jesus bearing our sorrows and carrying our pains. It's a powerful image that speaks to the depth of His love and the extent of His sacrifice on our behalf. And as I reflect on these words, I can't help but marvel at the profound implications they hold for our lives.

In Isaiah 53:3, the word "sorrows" in Hebrew actually means pains and grief. It's a reminder that Jesus didn't just carry our sins on the cross, but He also bore our sicknesses and carried our pains. It's a truth that brings me great comfort, knowing that whatever pain or illness I may face, Jesus has already borne it for me. He took it upon Himself so that I wouldn't have to carry it alone.

As I continue reading through the passage, I come across verse 5, which speaks of the chastisement Jesus endured for our peace. In Hebrew, the word "chastisement" means punishment, underscoring the severity of what Jesus endured on our behalf. And yet, despite the pain and suffering He endured, His ultimate goal was to bring us peace – a

THE CROSS

peace that surpasses all understanding and fills us with hope and assurance.

And it's not just any kind of peace – it's the Hebrew concept of "Shalom," which encompasses wholeness, safety, blessing, and prosperity. In other words, Jesus endured punishment so that we could experience complete wholeness and well-being in every area of our lives. It's a profound truth that speaks to the depth of His love and the lengths He was willing to go to ensure our restoration and healing.

So when I think about Jesus becoming sick on the cross, it's not just a historical event or a theological concept – it's a personal reality that has profound implications for my life. It's a reminder that His sacrifice wasn't limited to just one aspect of my being, but it encompassed every area of my existence – body, soul, and spirit. And as I meditate on this truth, I'm filled with gratitude and awe for the incredible love and compassion that Jesus has shown me, even in the midst of His own suffering.

You know, there's a verse in 1 Peter 2:24 that really challenges my perspective on healing and prayer. It's a passage that forces me to reconsider how I approach my own health and well-being in light of God's Word. In this verse, Peter makes a bold statement – he says that Jesus Himself bore our sins in His body on the cross, so that we might die to sin and live for righteousness. But then he goes even further and says that by His wounds, we have been healed.

> ***"He personally carried our sins in his body on the cross so that we can be dead to sin and live for what is right. By his wounds you are healed." 1 Peter 2:24***

Now, for a long time, I used to approach prayer for healing in a certain way. Whenever I or someone I cared about was sick or struggling with their health, my first instinct was to pray fervently for healing. I would plead with God to intervene, to miraculously heal the person and relieve their suffering. And while there's certainly nothing wrong with praying for healing, I've come to realize that there's a deeper truth at play here.

You see, Peter's words challenge me to shift my focus away from simply asking God for healing, and instead, to let His Word build me up and strengthen my faith. It's about meditating on the promises of God, standing firm on His Word, and boldly declaring what is rightfully ours as children of God. It's about recognizing that healing isn't just something we beg God for – it's something that has already been provided for us through the sacrifice of Jesus on the cross.

When Jesus bore our sins and sicknesses on the cross, He did so with the full knowledge of what it would mean for us. He knew that His wounds would be the source of our healing, that His suffering would bring us wholeness and restoration. And so, when we pray for healing, we're not begging God to do something He hasn't already done – we're simply claiming the promise that He has already made available to us through Jesus.

So as I reflect on 1 Peter 2:24, I'm reminded that my approach to prayer and healing needs to be grounded in faith and the truth of God's Word. Instead of approaching God with doubt and uncertainty, I can come to Him with confidence, knowing that He is faithful to fulfill His promises and bring healing to those who trust in Him. And so, I choose to stand firm on His Word, believing that by His wounds, I am healed.

It is easy to skim over certain passages in the Bible without really digging into their deeper meaning. But recently, I stumbled upon a verse that made me pause and reflect in a whole new way. It's found in Isaiah 53:3, and it talks about Jesus bearing our sorrows and pains. Now, when we hear the word "sorrows," we might think of emotional pain or grief. But in Hebrew, it actually refers to physical sickness.

THE CROSS

When I read this, it struck me – Jesus didn't just take on our sins on the cross, He also bore our sicknesses and carried our pains. This changes everything. Suddenly, the suffering of Jesus on the cross takes on a whole new depth of meaning. It's not just about forgiveness of sins, though that's incredibly important. It's also about physical healing and restoration.

You see, Jesus didn't become sick on the cross because He deserved it or because He had done anything wrong. No, He willingly took on our sickness and pain so that we could be healed and made whole. It's a profound act of love and sacrifice that demonstrates the depth of God's compassion for us.

And when I think about it, it makes perfect sense. Jesus came to earth to bring wholeness and restoration to every aspect of our lives – body, soul, and spirit. He didn't just want to save us from our sins; He wanted to bring healing and freedom in every area of our lives.

So why did Jesus become sick? Simply put, it was for our sake. It was so that we could experience the fullness of His healing power and be restored to health and wholeness. And that's a truth that I'll hold onto tightly, especially in those moments when sickness and pain seem overwhelming.

Have you ever thought about why Jesus, who is often depicted as majestic and powerful, would willingly choose to become poor? It's a question that might seem puzzling at first, but when we delve into the Scriptures, we discover a profound truth hidden beneath the surface.

In 2 Corinthians 8:9, Paul writes about this very topic, stating that *"though Jesus was rich, He became poor for our sake."* Now, when we hear the word "poor," we might immediately think of financial lack or material deprivation. But in this context, it goes much deeper than that.

JESUS: MY ROLE MODEL

"For you know the grace of our Lord Jesus Christ, that though He was rich, yet for your sakes He became poor, that you through His poverty might become rich." **2 Corinthians 8:9**

Jesus didn't become poor in the sense of lacking material possessions or wealth. No, He became poor in the sense of relinquishing the glory and splendor of His heavenly throne to dwell among us as a humble carpenter's son. He laid aside His divine privileges and took on the form of a servant, living a life marked by humility and simplicity.

But why would Jesus do such a thing? Why would the King of kings choose to embrace poverty and humility? The answer lies in the very heart of His mission on earth. Jesus became poor so that we might become rich.

Now, when we talk about riches in the context of our relationship with God, we're not just talking about material wealth or possessions. We're talking about a richness of blessings, a richness of grace, and a richness of spiritual inheritance that far surpasses anything this world could offer.

When Jesus became poor, He paved the way for us to experience true abundance – not just in terms of material provision, but in every area of our lives. Through His poverty, we have been given access to the riches of His grace and the abundance of His kingdom.

So, why did Jesus become poor? It was all for our sake – so that we might experience the fullness of His blessings and the richness of His love. And that's a truth worth celebrating and embracing with grateful hearts.

Paul understood something that goes beyond our ordinary understanding of time and history. He grasped the idea that the work of the cross wasn't just a one-time event that happened in the past and was finished. No, he saw it as something eternal, something that transcends our linear concept of time.

THE CROSS

Paul talked about making up in his own body what is lacking in the sufferings of Christ. Now, at first glance, that might sound a bit confusing. How could anything be lacking in the sufferings of Christ? Didn't He endure enough on the cross?

But Paul wasn't suggesting that Jesus' sacrifice was incomplete or insufficient. Instead, he was highlighting the ongoing impact and relevance of the cross in our lives today. He saw the cross as not just a historical event, but as a timeless reality that continues to shape and transform us.

And Paul wasn't alone in this understanding. Throughout the Bible, there are hints and glimpses of Jesus in eternity – moments when His divine nature breaks through the fabric of time and space. It's as if the cross, with all its profound implications, reverberates throughout eternity, shaping the very fabric of reality itself.

So when Paul talks about bearing in our bodies the dying of Jesus, he's not just talking about physical suffering or martyrdom. He's talking about a spiritual reality – the ongoing work of the cross in our lives, as we die to ourselves and allow the life of Jesus to be revealed in us.

It's a challenging concept to wrap our minds around, but it's also incredibly liberating. Because it means that the cross isn't just a distant event from the past. It's a living, breathing reality that continues to unfold in our lives today, bringing healing, transformation, and eternal significance to everything we do. And that's something worth pondering and embracing with awe and gratitude.

When I read about Jesus being referred to as the "Lamb slain before the foundation of the world," it's like peering into the depths of eternity itself. It's a concept that stretches my understanding of time and space, yet it speaks to the profound and timeless nature of Christ's sacrifice.

Peter's words in his letter hit me deeply. He talks about how we've been ransomed from the futile ways passed down through generations, not with things like silver or gold, but with the precious blood of Christ. It's as if he's reminding us of the immeasurable value of what Jesus did for us on the cross.

The idea that Jesus was destined for this sacrifice even before the world was formed is mind-boggling. It's like God had this eternal plan in motion, knowing full well what would be required to redeem humanity from sin and brokenness. And yet, it was revealed to us in a specific moment in history, at the end of times, for our sake.

It's a paradoxical truth – that the work of Christ on the cross is both a historical event, rooted in space-time, and an eternal reality, stretching beyond the confines of our understanding. It's a reminder that God's love and redemption extend far beyond the limits of our comprehension.

And in this mysterious interplay between eternity and time, between God and humans, we catch a glimpse of the depth of God's suffering for us. It's as if a part of God Himself suffers eternally for our sins, bearing the weight of our brokenness and rebellion.

So, while we affirm that the work of Christ on the cross is finished and complete, we also recognize the ongoing significance of His sacrifice throughout eternity. It's a profound mystery that invites us to awe and wonder, reminding us of the immeasurable depth of God's love for us.

As I explore Scripture, I'm confronted with the truth that God, in His holiness, must also be just. He can't tolerate evil lingering in His presence indefinitely. Those who persistently reject His mercy find themselves in a state of eternal separation from Him, facing the consequences of their rebellion in a place of unending punishment. It's a sobering reality, one that speaks to the seriousness of our choices and the gravity of God's righteous judgment.

As I reflect on this, I can't help but imagine the anguish God must experience when His beloved children turn away from Him. Like any loving parent, His heart must ache at the thought of His children choosing paths that lead to pain, harm, and self-destruction. It's a pain that cuts deep, infinitely deeper than any human parent could ever fathom.

And yet, in the midst of this sorrow, God's love remains steadfast. He longs to pour out His grace and mercy upon us, to draw us back into His embrace. But when we persist in our rebellion, when we refuse to heed His call to repentance, it must grieve Him deeply.

In contemplating the suffering of God, I'm reminded of the incomparable pain that Christ endured on the cross. He bore the weight of all our sins, past, present, and future, experiencing the full extent of human suffering and separation from God. There's no depth of anguish that Christ hasn't already plumbed, no pain He hasn't already borne on our behalf.

And yet, even in the midst of His suffering, Christ's sacrifice speaks of God's boundless love for us. It's a love that seeks to woo us back into relationship, to draw us near with cords of kindness and compassion. As Paul reminds us, it's God's kindness that leads us to repentance, beckoning us to turn from our sin and embrace His grace.

So, as I consider these profound truths, I'm filled with gratitude for the kingdom that God offers us – a kingdom that cannot be shaken, a kingdom built on the unshakable foundation of His love and righteousness. And in response, I'm compelled to offer God the worship He deserves – worship that is marked by reverence and awe, recognizing Him as the consuming fire of love that burns away our sin and purifies our hearts.

As I reflect on the profound significance of Jesus' sacrifice on the cross, I'm struck by the depth of His love and the magnitude of His grace. In those agonizing moments, He willingly took upon Himself the weight of our sin, becoming sin itself so that we might be made righteous in the eyes of God. It's a truth that humbles me and fills me with awe, knowing that Jesus endured such agony for my sake.

But it doesn't stop there. Jesus also became a curse for us, bearing the punishment that we rightfully deserved. He suffered the consequences of our rebellion so that we might be set free from the curse of sin and death, experiencing the fullness of God's blessings and provision.

And in His suffering, Jesus also bore our sicknesses and infirmities, carrying our pains so that we might be healed and made whole. His stripes became the means of our restoration, bringing us into a place of health and wholeness that transcends physical ailments and touches the depths of our souls.

Furthermore, Jesus became poor so that we might become rich – not just in material wealth, but in spiritual abundance and eternal blessings. His poverty became our prosperity, as He laid aside His heavenly riches to offer us the incomparable wealth of His grace and salvation.

In light of these truths, I'm reminded of the immeasurable depth of God's love for us. Through Jesus' sacrificial death on the cross, we are given the opportunity to experience forgiveness, redemption, healing, and abundance beyond measure. It's a gift that I can never fully comprehend or repay, but one that I gratefully receive with a heart overflowing with thanksgiving.

As I ponder these four major aspects of Jesus' work on the cross – His bearing of sin, His becoming a curse, His taking on sickness, and His embracing of poverty – I'm compelled to respond with worship, gratitude, and surrender. May my life be a living testimony to the transformative power of the cross, and may I never cease to marvel at the wonder of God's redeeming love displayed through the sacrifice of His Son.

THE CROSS

HELL

Growing up, I had heard the story countless times—the tale of a man who walked the dusty roads of ancient Israel, healing the sick, comforting the brokenhearted, and speaking words that stirred the hearts of those who listened. His name was Jesus, and His life was a beacon of hope in a world overshadowed by suffering and uncertainty.

As a child, I listened wide-eyed to the stories of Jesus feeding thousands with a few loaves and fishes, of Him calming storms with a mere command, and of His compassion for the outcasts and sinners. It seemed like a tale of wonder and miracles, of a man who defied the natural order of things.

But as I grew older, I began to understand that Jesus' life was not just a collection of miraculous events. It was leading to something much deeper and more profound—a purpose that would change the course of human history forever.

The pivotal moment in Jesus' life, and indeed in all of human existence, was His death on a cross. It was an event that defied logic and human understanding. How could a man so full of life and goodness be condemned to such a brutal and humiliating death?

The death of Christ, which I had learned about from childhood Sunday school lessons and later through deep study of the Scriptures, was not just a tragic end to a remarkable life. It was the fulfillment of a divine plan—a plan that was set in motion long before Jesus was born in Bethlehem.

The death of Christ was foretold by prophets centuries before His birth. Isaiah spoke of Him as the suffering servant who would bear the sins of many (Isaiah 53). The Psalms foretold His betrayal, His crucifixion, and even His resurrection (Psalm 22; Psalm 69). These prophecies, once cryptic and mysterious to me, now revealed the intricate tapestry of God's redemptive plan.

As I delve deeper into the events leading to Jesus' death—the Last Supper, His agonizing prayer in the Garden of Gethsemane, the betrayal by Judas, the trials before Pilate and Herod, the mocking, the scourging, and the agonizing journey to Golgotha—I am struck by the enormity of His sacrifice.

Jesus, the Son of God, willingly laid down His life for the sins of humanity. He endured unimaginable suffering, not because of His own wrongdoing, but out of love for us. His death was the ultimate act of selflessness and obedience to His Father's will.

As I reflect on the events of that fateful day, when darkness shrouded the earth from the sixth to the ninth hour, I'm reminded of the profound symbolism embedded in those hours of gloom. Darkness isn't merely the absence of light; it's a poignant symbol of evil and the spiritual battle that raged as Jesus hung on the cross.

During those agonizing hours, Jesus experienced something incomprehensible. As the weight of humanity's sins bore down upon Him, He cried out, *"My God, my God, why have you forsaken me?"*

(Matthew 27:46). In that moment, Jesus, the sinless Son of God, was separated from His Father. It wasn't just a physical separation; it was a spiritual chasm that He willingly endured for our sake.

Scripture tells us that Jesus descended to the realm of the dead, known as Hades or Sheol (Acts 2:27). This wasn't a place of torment for Jesus but rather a place where the righteous dead awaited their redemption. It was here that Jesus proclaimed His victory over sin and death (1 Peter 3:18-19). He liberated those who had been held captive, fulfilling the prophecy that He would lead captivity captive (Ephesians 4:8-10).

In the heart of the earth, during those three days and nights, Jesus was actively engaged in the work of redemption. He wasn't passive; He was proclaiming His triumph, setting the stage for His ultimate victory over sin and death. His journey through Hades wasn't aimless; it was purposeful, fulfilling the divine plan of salvation that had been set in motion before the foundation of the world.

As I ponder these profound truths, I'm struck by the depth of Jesus' love and the extent of His sacrifice. He didn't just die for our sins on the cross; He descended into the depths of darkness to ensure that every aspect of our brokenness would be redeemed. His journey through Hades underscores His victory over sin and death, offering hope and salvation to all who believe in Him.

The darkness that enveloped the earth during those hours wasn't just a cosmic phenomenon; it was a tangible reminder of the spiritual battle that Jesus fought on our behalf. It was a battle that He won decisively, emerging triumphant on the third day when He rose from the dead, defeating death and securing eternal life for all who trust in Him.

As I contemplate where Jesus went during those three days and nights, I'm filled with gratitude and awe. His journey through the heart of the earth wasn't just a necessary step in the fulfillment of prophecy;

HELL

it was a powerful demonstration of His love and His commitment to rescue humanity from sin and darkness. He willingly entered the depths so that we could be lifted up into the light of His salvation.

As I delve into the depths of Scripture, exploring the concept of Hades and its implications, I'm struck by the various terms used to describe the realms beyond our earthly existence. Hades, mentioned eleven times in the New Testament, is often associated with a place of the dead, a temporary abode before the final judgment. It's a concept that challenges our understanding of the afterlife and the spiritual dimensions beyond our sight.

In Matthew 11:23, Jesus speaks of Hades as a place of punishment, situated below the earth. This imagery paints a picture of separation and consequence, where the wicked are held to account for their deeds. The gravity of this place is underscored in Matthew 16:18, where Hades is depicted as an enemy, a realm diametrically opposed to the kingdom of God, reserved for those who reject His grace.

A poignant illustration of Hades is found in Luke 16:19-26, where Jesus shares the parable of the rich man and Lazarus. Here, Hades is described as a place of torment and flame, contrasting sharply with Abraham's bosom, a place of comfort and peace for the righteous. This parable not only highlights the stark realities of life after death but also emphasizes the eternal consequences of our choices on earth.

The temporal nature of Hades becomes evident in Acts 2:22-31, where Peter refers to the prophecy of David regarding the Messiah. Jesus, though crucified and buried, did not remain in Hades; instead, He conquered death and rose victorious. His resurrection affirmed His victory over sin and Hades, offering hope of eternal life to all who believe in Him.

Beyond Hades, Scripture introduces other terms such as Tartarus, mentioned in 2 Peter 2:4, as a place reserved for angels who sinned. This signifies a unique realm of punishment distinct from Hades, underscoring the divine justice administered according to God's sovereign will.

The lake of fire, mentioned in Revelation 20:13-14, represents the final destination for Hades and all those who reject God's redemption. This eternal lake signifies the second death, a complete separation from God's presence and eternal damnation for those whose names are not written in the Book of Life.

Gehenna, often translated as hell, is another term used by Jesus in Matthew 10:28 and Mark 9:43. It symbolizes a place of fiery judgment, emphasizing the seriousness of sin and its consequences. It serves as a warning of the eternal punishment awaiting those who persist in rebellion against God.

The abyss, referenced in Revelation 9:12 and 20:13, is a place associated with demonic forces and represents a realm of spiritual darkness and torment. Demons fear being consigned to this abyss, highlighting its dread and the authority of God over spiritual realms.

Reflecting on these scriptural truths about Hades and its related concepts, I'm reminded of the importance of our choices in this life. Each term paints a vivid picture of spiritual realities beyond our comprehension, urging us to seek God's grace and salvation through Jesus Christ. His death and resurrection offer us a pathway to eternal life in His presence, far from the darkness and torment of Hades and its associated realms.

HELL

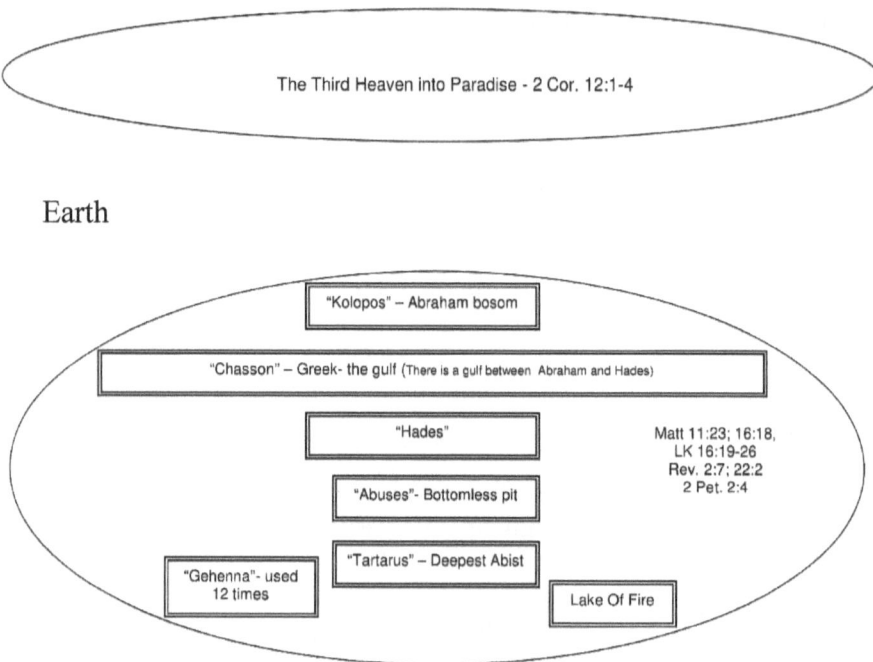

As I ponder the profound mystery of Jesus spending three days and three nights in the heart of the earth, I find myself drawn into a deeper contemplation of His sacrificial journey for humanity's redemption. In Matthew 12:40, Jesus Himself draws a parallel to the prophet Jonah, who spent three days and three nights in the belly of a great fish. This comparison serves not only as a sign of Jesus' authority but also foreshadows His own death, burial, and resurrection.

Seventy-two hours. That's the time frame we're talking about here. Jesus, the Son of God, who walked among us in human form, willingly endured the agony of the cross. His body was taken down from the cruel instrument of torture and laid in a tomb. This wasn't just any burial; it marked the pivotal moment in history when God's plan for salvation reached its climactic fulfillment.

Imagine the silence that must have settled over Jerusalem as Jesus' lifeless body was carried to the tomb. The disciples, still reeling from the events of the crucifixion, struggles with grief and confusion. Those who witnessed His miracles and teachings now faced the stark reality of His absence. For them, hope seemed lost, and the promise of a Messiah appeared shattered.

Yet, in that stillness, a profound spiritual battle raged. As Jesus lay in the heart of the earth, a realm unseen by human eyes, His spirit was engaged in a mission far greater than any earthly conflict. Ephesians 4:8-10 hints at this cosmic victory, where Jesus descended into the lower parts of the earth, leading captivity captive and triumphing over the forces of darkness.

Three days and nights. It was during this time that Jesus bridged the gap between heaven and earth, fulfilling the ancient prophecies and promises of God. Hebrews 9:11-12 describes how Jesus, as the ultimate High Priest, entered the Most Holy Place once and for all, not with the blood of goats and calves, but with His own blood, securing eternal redemption for all who believe in Him.

The significance of those 72 hours cannot be overstated. They represent the culmination of God's plan to reconcile humanity to Himself through the atoning sacrifice of His Son. Jesus' death was not merely a tragic event; it was the pivotal moment that shattered the power of sin and death, offering humanity a pathway to forgiveness and eternal life.

As I reflect on Matthew 12:40 and the profound symbolism it holds, I am reminded of the depth of God's love and the lengths to which He went to rescue us. Jesus' descent into the heart of the earth was a journey of unimaginable suffering and unparalleled grace. It was through His death and resurrection that He conquered sin and Hades, offering us the gift of salvation and the hope of eternal life in Him.

As I delve into the profound mysteries surrounding Jesus' journey into Hades, I'm confronted with Scriptures, revealing layers of spiritual truth that transcend time and space. Ephesians 4:8 captures this beautifully, speaking of Jesus descending into the lower parts of the earth before ascending triumphantly to the heights of heaven. This descent, as Acts 2:22-31 describes, was not merely a physical death but a spiritual descent into the heart of the earth—Hades itself.

In Luke 23:43, amidst the agony of crucifixion, Jesus uttered words of profound promise to the repentant thief beside Him: "*Today you will be with me in paradise.*" This "today" is not bound by earthly time but signifies an immediate transition to paradise, the third heaven where God dwells. It underscores the assurance of eternal life given to those who believe in Him, even in the midst of His descent into the depths of Hades.

Ephesians 4:8-10 sheds light on the spiritual realm Jesus navigated during His descent. He led captivity captive, liberating those who were held in Abraham's bosom—the righteous of the Old Testament era awaiting the Messiah's redemptive work. This act symbolizes Jesus' victory over sin and death, culminating in His ascension to heaven, where He now reigns in glory.

Romans 10:6-7 hints at Christ's profound journey even into the Abyss, the bottomless pit—a realm associated with demonic forces and profound darkness. This descent into the lower parts of the earth fulfilled Isaiah 53:8-9,12, where Jesus was numbered with the transgressors and suffered with the wicked in Hades, fulfilling the prophecy of Psalm 88, where His suffering and descent into the depths are poetically lamented.

Matthew 12:40 draws a striking parallel between Jesus' ordeal and Jonah's time in the belly of the great fish. Just as Jonah's experience prefigured Jesus' death, burial, and resurrection, Psalm 68 and 69 vividly depict Jesus' anguish and deliverance in Hades, echoed in Revelation 9:1-2,11, where He confronts the forces of darkness and triumphs over them.

Reflecting on these passages, I am humbled by the depth of Jesus' sacrifice and His victory over sin and death. His descent into Hades was not just a journey through darkness but a triumphant march, liberating souls and proclaiming His ultimate victory. It underscores His role as the Redeemer who bridged the gap between God and humanity, offering salvation and eternal life to all who believe.

I find myself drawn into the profound and mysterious journey of Jesus into Hades—a journey that spans the depths of human suffering and the heights of divine victory. As I explore the Scriptures that illuminate this journey, I am captivated by the layers of meaning and significance they reveal.

Ephesians 4:8 begins this exploration, describing Jesus' descent into the lower parts of the earth before His triumphant ascent to heaven. This descent, as Acts 2:22-31 further details, took Jesus into Hades, the realm of the dead, where His soul traversed realms unseen by mortal eyes.

Luke 23:43 offers a poignant moment amidst Jesus' crucifixion. To the repentant thief, Jesus promises, "Today you will be with me in paradise." This declaration transcends earthly time, affirming immediate fellowship in the presence of God—a promise fulfilled even as Jesus descended into the depths of Hades.

Ephesians 4:8-10 continues to shed light on this spiritual journey. Jesus, after His death on the cross, led captivity captive—liberating the righteous souls who awaited redemption in Abraham's bosom. This act signifies His victory over sin and death, culminating in His ascension to heaven, where He now reigns as Lord.

Romans 10:6-7 and Isaiah 53:8-9,12 provide prophetic insights into Jesus' descent into Hades. He was numbered with the transgressors, suffering alongside the wicked, fulfilling the Old Testament prophecies that foretold His sacrificial death and descent into the realm of the dead.

Matthew 12:40 draws a parallel between Jesus' experience and that of Jonah, who spent three days and nights in the belly of the great fish. Just as Jonah foreshadowed Jesus' death, burial, and resurrection, so too did Jesus descend into Hades, confronting the powers of darkness and triumphing over them.

Psalms 68 and 69 poetically depict Jesus' suffering and deliverance in Hades, anticipating His victory over death and His ultimate triumph. Revelation 9:1-2,11 further underscores Jesus' authority over the Abyss, where He confronts the forces of evil and asserts His sovereignty.

Contemplating these Scriptures, I am struck by the depth of Jesus' sacrifice and the extent of His love for humanity. His journey into Hades was not merely a descent into darkness but a victorious mission to liberate souls and proclaim His triumph over sin and death. It reveals His role as the Redeemer who bridged the gap between heaven and earth, offering salvation and eternal life to all who believe in Him.

The Scriptures paint a vivid picture of Jesus' descent into Hades—a journey marked by suffering, triumph, and ultimate victory. His death and resurrection are not only historical events but profound acts of redemption that forever changed the course of human history. As I reflect on these truths, I am reminded of the magnitude of God's plan for salvation and the unmatched love demonstrated through Jesus Christ, who willingly descended into the depths to offer us eternal life.

As I explore the profound purpose of Christ's death, I'm struck by the clarity and depth with which Scripture reveals this central truth. Jesus Himself declared during the institution of the Lord's Supper, "*This is my blood of the covenant, which is poured out for many for the forgiveness of sins*" (Matthew 26:28). These words resonate through generations, marking the memorial of His sacrificial death as a profound act securing forgiveness for all who believe.

In Mark 10:45, Jesus underscores His mission: "*The Son of Man came not to be served but to serve, and to give his life as a ransom for many.*" This ransom, a payment to liberate us from the bondage of sin, highlights His selfless act of atonement. John 10:15 further reinforces this truth: "I lay down my life for the sheep." Here, Jesus portrays Himself as the sacrificial lamb whose death brings salvation to His flock.

Reflecting on John 10:17-18, I see Jesus' voluntary surrender of His life for the sake of humanity: "No one takes it from me, but I lay it down of my own accord." His death was not a tragic end imposed upon Him but a deliberate act of love and obedience to the Father's will.

In the encounter with Nicodemus, Jesus dismisses the notion of merely being a teacher sent from God, emphasizing the necessity of spiritual rebirth to enter the kingdom of God (John 3:1-21). His death wasn't about receiving accolades or pity; as Luke 23:28-31 reveals, even amidst His suffering, Jesus redirects the focus to the deeper significance of His sacrifice for the salvation of souls.

The tearing of the temple veil at the moment of Jesus' death (Matthew 27:51) symbolizes the profound truth that through His sacrificial death, the barrier between humanity and God's presence was forever removed. This act signifies that access to God is now available to all who come through faith in Christ, not through rituals or human effort.

The apostle Paul expounds on this foundational truth in his writings. In Galatians 3:13, he declares that Christ redeemed us from the curse of the law by becoming a curse for us. This substitutionary atonement is further elucidated in 2 Corinthians 5:21, where Paul explains that God made Christ, who knew no sin, to be sin on our behalf, so that in Him we might become the righteousness of God.

The centrality of Christ's death for our sins is echoed throughout Paul's letters. In 1 Corinthians 15:3, Paul emphasizes that Christ died for our sins according to the Scriptures, fulfilling the prophetic promises of the Old Testament. Romans 3:25 describes Jesus as the propitiation for our sins through faith in His blood, highlighting His role in satisfying God's righteous wrath against sin.

Paul's resolve to preach "Jesus Christ and him crucified" (1 Corinthians 2:2) underscores the foundational importance of Christ's death in the proclamation of the gospel. It is through His death, burial, and resurrection that the power of sin is broken, and reconciliation with God is made possible for all who believe.

The Scriptures resound with the profound truth that Christ's death was not incidental but intentional, securing forgiveness and reconciliation for humanity. His sacrificial death fulfilled the divine plan of redemption, offering salvation to all who put their trust in Him. This truth transforms my understanding of God's love and grace, compelling me to embrace the significance of Christ's death as the cornerstone of my faith and the gateway to eternal life.

As I meditate on the profound truth of Christ's sacrificial death, I am drawn to the powerful declarations of Scripture that illuminate its significance. Peter, in his epistle, encapsulates this truth succinctly: "Christ also suffered for sins once, the righteous for the unrighteous, that He might bring us to God" (1 Peter 3:18). This verse underscores the essential purpose of Christ's death—to reconcile humanity to God through His perfect sacrifice.

Peter continues to emphasize this truth in 1 Peter 2:24, proclaiming that Christ "*bore our sins in His body on the tree,*" highlighting the personal and sacrificial nature of His atonement. These words resonate deeply, reminding me that every sin, every failing, was laid upon Him, so that we might be made right with God.

Turning to the words of John in 1 John 1:7, I find reassurance in the cleansing power of Jesus' blood: "*The blood of Jesus His Son cleanses us from all sin.*" This cleansing is not partial or temporary but complete and eternal, purifying us completely from every stain of sin. John further affirms in 1 John 2:2 that Jesus is the propitiation for our sins, the satisfaction of God's righteous requirement for atonement.

The author of Hebrews succinctly captures the necessity of blood for forgiveness in Hebrews 9:22: "*Without the shedding of blood there is no forgiveness of sins.*" This foundational principle underscores the seriousness of sin and the costly remedy provided through Christ's sacrifice. Moreover, Hebrews 9:26 reveals the culmination of God's redemptive plan in Christ, who appeared "*to put away sin by the sacrifice of Himself,*" bringing about eternal reconciliation between God and humanity.

Even in the prophetic words of Isaiah 53, written centuries before Christ's birth, the sacrificial nature of His death is foretold with striking clarity. Isaiah paints a poignant picture of the suffering Messiah: "*He was pierced for our transgressions; he was crushed for our iniquities*" (Isaiah 53:5). These verses vividly portray the substitutionary atonement of Christ, who bore the punishment that rightfully belonged to us, securing our peace and healing through His stripes.

Reflecting on the Old Testament sacrificial system, where innocent lambs were offered as sin offerings, I recognize its profound foreshadowing of Christ's ultimate sacrifice. The lamb, chosen for its innocence and value, served as a powerful symbol of the One who would come to bear the sins of the world. John the Baptist aptly identified Jesus as "*the Lamb of God, who takes away the sin of the world*" (John 1:29), aligning Him with the sacrificial lamb whose blood would bring redemption.

Peter reinforces this imagery in 1 Peter 1:18-19, contrasting the perishable nature of silver and gold with the preciousness of Christ's blood, likening it to "*a lamb without blemish or spot.*" This analogy underscores the purity and priceless value of Jesus' sacrificial death, which redeems us from sin's bondage.

In the Book of Revelation, the redeemed are depicted as those who have washed their robes and made them white in the blood of the Lamb (Revelation 7:14). This imagery signifies the cleansing power of Christ's blood, which purifies and sanctifies all who believe in Him.

Ultimately, Christ's sacrificial death reveals His unparalleled love and mercy toward humanity. His willingness to lay down His life demonstrates His gentleness and tenderness, contrasting sharply with the unprovoked hostility He faced. As I contemplate these truths, I am humbled by the depth of God's love displayed through Jesus' sacrificial death—a love that offers forgiveness, redemption, and eternal life to all who trust in Him.

JESUS *is* ALIVE!

    I still remember that Sunday morning like it was yesterday. The sun was just beginning to rise, casting a gentle glow over the sleepy town. As I sat with my coffee, the air filled with the sounds of birds singing their morning chorus, I couldn't help but reflect on the incredible significance of that day over two thousand years ago—the day Jesus Christ rose from the dead. It was a quiet, almost ordinary moment that belied the extraordinary event we were celebrating: the resurrection of Jesus Christ.

    Growing up, the story of the resurrection was always part of my life. Every Easter, my family would gather around the table, and my father would share the story with us. He had a way of telling it that made the events come alive. He would talk about the women going to the tomb early in the morning, hearts heavy with grief, only to find the stone rolled away and the tomb empty. It was in those moments, with the smell of freshly baked bread in the air and the sunlight streaming through the windows, that I began to grasp the profound mystery of the resurrection.

    I remember one Easter in particular, when I was about fifteen years old. My parents had taken me to a sunrise service at the local church

JESUS IS ALIVE!

where my uncle and his family was going. As we stood in church, bundled up against the early morning chill, the pastor spoke about the resurrection with a passion that stirred something deep within me. He talked about how Jesus' resurrection wasn't just a miraculous event in the past, but a living reality that continues to transform lives today. It was in that cold morning air, surrounded by people singing and praying, that I first felt the resurrection as a personal and powerful truth.

The resurrection of Jesus Christ is not just a story we tell once a year; it's the cornerstone of our faith, the defining moment that gives meaning and hope to everything we believe. It's the ultimate proof that love is stronger than death, that light can conquer even the darkest of nights. It's the assurance that no matter how hopeless things might seem, there is always the promise of new life and new beginnings.

As I've grown older, the resurrection has taken on even greater significance in my life. I've faced my own share of dark days and seemingly insurmountable challenges. But in those moments, I've found comfort and strength in the knowledge that Jesus overcame the ultimate obstacle—death itself. His resurrection is a powerful reminder that no matter how bleak things may look, there is always hope for a new dawn, a fresh start.

These moments at the empty tomb were not just the culmination of a divine plan but the beginning of a new era. They marked the transition from despair to hope, from death to life. Jesus' resurrection was not just a victory over physical death; it was the promise of eternal life, a new covenant sealed with His own blood. The resurrection was the cornerstone of faith, a testament to the power of God and the promise of redemption.

Reflecting on these events, I am struck by the profound love and grace that underpin them. Jesus' willingness to endure death and separation from the Father, only to rise victorious, is a testament to His boundless love for humanity. It is a love that reaches across time and space, touching each of us in our moments of doubt and fear, and lifting us up with the promise of new life.

The resurrection of Jesus Christ is not just an event in history; it is a living, breathing reality that continues to inspire and transform lives. It is a beacon of hope that shines through the darkest nights, a reminder that no matter how deep the sorrow, joy comes in the morning. As I ponder the empty tomb and the risen Christ, I am filled with a sense of awe and gratitude, knowing that because He lives, I too can face whatever challenges come my way with hope and confidence.

I think back to those early disciples, huddled together in fear and uncertainty after Jesus' crucifixion. They had followed Him, believed in Him, and now He was gone. I can imagine their despair, their hearts heavy with sorrow and confusion. And then, the unimaginable happened: Jesus appeared to them, alive, just as He had promised. The joy and wonder they must have felt in that moment is something I try to carry with me every day. It's a reminder that Jesus' resurrection is not just a historical event, but a living reality that continues to bring hope and transformation to our world.

One of the most powerful aspects of the resurrection for me is the way it connects the past with the present and the future. It's a bridge that spans time, linking the first Easter morning with every moment of our lives. When I face challenges or uncertainties, I remind myself of the resurrection, and it gives me the courage to move forward. It's a testament to the power of faith and the enduring promise of God's love.

The resurrection is also a call to action. It's a reminder that we are called to live out the hope and joy of Easter in our daily lives. It's about more than just believing in a miraculous event; it's about allowing that belief to shape who we are and how we live. It's about being a light in the darkness, a source of hope for others, just as the resurrection is for us.

JESUS IS ALIVE!

As I continue my journey of faith, I am constantly reminded of the transformative power of the resurrection. It's a story that never grows old, a truth that never loses its power. It's a living reality that shapes my life in profound ways, guiding me, inspiring me, and giving me hope for the future.

So, as I sit here, the sun climbing higher in the sky and the day beginning to unfold, I am filled with a deep sense of gratitude and wonder for the resurrection of Jesus Christ. It's a story that has touched my life in countless ways, and one that I will carry with me always. It's a reminder that no matter what challenges I may face, I can face them with the confidence and hope that comes from knowing that Jesus has risen, and that through Him, I have the promise of new life and new beginnings.

I can only imagine the evening sky in Jerusalem on that Saturday was a deep canvas of stars, the kind of night that makes you ponder the mysteries of existence. I always find something almost sacred in those twilight hours, a time when the hustle of the day has died down and a tranquil hush blankets the city. It's a time for reflection, a time to contemplate the incredible events that unfolded in that very place over two thousand years ago. As the clock struck 6:00 PM, the beginning of a new day according to Jewish tradition, it marked the start of something extraordinary: the resurrection of Jesus Christ.

You can only imagine that moment where the world lay in a state of quiet anticipation, the air thick with the promise of a new dawn. Jesus, who had been crucified and buried, was about to rise from the dead, a triumphant act that would forever change the course of history. In that divine moment, He was justified, made alive, and raised from the dead, not just in a physical sense, but as a testament to His victory over sin and death.

As I picture it, I can see the forces of darkness trembling, their power stripped away by the sheer magnitude of what was happening. Jesus, standing victorious in the very heart of hell, proclaiming His triumph. I often wonder about the reactions of those demonic powers, once so confident in their hold over humanity, now faced with the undeniable truth that they had been defeated. Jesus had descended into the depths of Hades, not as a victim, but as a conqueror, bringing a message of victory and liberation.

One of the most astonishing aspects of this event is what happened next. The Old Testament saints, those faithful souls who had long awaited the fulfillment of God's promise, were raised from their graves. Matthew 27:51-53 tells us that after Jesus' resurrection, many of these saints appeared to people in Jerusalem. Just imagine the shock and awe of seeing figures from the past, figures you had only read about in sacred texts, now walking the streets, living testimonies to the power of resurrection. It's a scene that defies all logic, yet it happened, further underscoring the reality that Jesus had indeed conquered death.

I often find myself reflecting on what it must have been like for Jesus to ascend into heaven, His mission on earth accomplished. During the forty days following His resurrection, He appeared to His disciples, as Paul recounts in 1 Corinthians 15:6, and to more than five hundred others, including a momentous encounter on the road to Emmaus. These appearances weren't just fleeting glimpses; they were profound, life-altering experiences that left no doubt in the minds of those who witnessed them that Jesus was alive.

In those forty days, Jesus continued to teach and guide His followers, giving them commands and preparing them for the monumental task ahead. I can't help but marvel at the thought of Him, surrounded by the cloud of witnesses, ascending into heaven, His earthly mission complete but His work far from finished. It's a powerful image, one that fills me with a sense of awe and a deep sense of purpose.

The resurrection wasn't just a moment in time; it was the beginning of a new era. Jesus didn't just rise from the dead; He ushered in a new

JESUS IS ALIVE!

way of life, a new reality where death no longer held the final word. He didn't just conquer the grave; He opened the door to eternal life, a life that begins here and now and extends into the infinite beyond.

And then there's the sprinkling of His blood in heaven, an act that purified everything, that restored what was broken and made all things new. It's a concept that might seem abstract or distant, but for me, it's deeply personal. It's the assurance that through Jesus' sacrifice and resurrection, I am made new, that the brokenness in my life is not the end of the story, but the beginning of something beautiful and whole.

As I ponder the resurrection, I am filled with a profound sense of gratitude. Jesus' resurrection is not just a historical fact; it's a living, breathing reality that continues to shape my life in ways I can't even begin to fully comprehend. It's a reminder that no matter how dark the night, there is always the promise of a new day, a new beginning. It's the cornerstone of my faith, the source of my hope, and the reason I believe that nothing is impossible with God.

In those quiet moments, as I sit and reflect on the resurrection, I am reminded of the incredible gift we have been given. The resurrection is not just a story to be told; it's a truth to be lived, a reality that calls us to walk in the light of new life and new possibilities. It's a call to live with courage and hope, knowing that just as Jesus was raised, we too can rise above our circumstances and walk in the victory that He has won for us.

When I think about Jesus' journey through death and resurrection, it's more than just a theological concept or an event in history. It's deeply personal, a story that touches the very core of my being. To imagine what He endured, the depths of His suffering, and the magnitude of His triumph, is to grasp the very essence of faith and hope.

Jesus experienced two profound and distinct deaths. The first was a spiritual death, a separation from the Father that is beyond my full comprehension. It's hard to even fathom what that must have felt like.

JESUS: MY ROLE MODEL

Imagine the most painful separation you've ever experienced, the kind that leaves a gaping void in your heart. Now magnify that a thousand-fold, because this was no ordinary relationship; this was the Son of God, who had been in perfect communion with the Father for all eternity, now experiencing a chasm so vast it must have felt like an endless abyss.

This separation was a result of Jesus becoming sin. Not that He sinned, but He took on our sin, bearing the weight of all our wrongdoings. In that moment, He became the embodiment of all that is wrong in the world, experiencing the full brunt of divine justice. For those three dark days and nights, He suffered in hell, a place of torment and utter desolation, so that we would never have to.

I often reflect on those agonizing moments and what it must have been like for Jesus to be utterly alone, cut off from the Father's love. It's a sobering thought, one that fills me with both sorrow and gratitude. Sorrow, because it was my sin that placed Him there, and gratitude, because He chose to endure it for my sake. It's a kind of love that is hard to wrap my head around, a love that defies logic and transcends understanding.

Then there was His physical death, a brutal, painful end on the cross. It was the culmination of His earthly ministry, a death that signified the ultimate sacrifice. His body, broken and battered, bore the marks of our rebellion. But even in His physical death, there was hope, because it wasn't the end of the story. His death was a passage to something greater, a gateway to resurrection and new life.

First Timothy 3:16 captures the essence of this profound mystery: "God was manifest in the flesh," referring to the Incarnation, where God became human in the person of Jesus Christ. He walked among us, experienced our joys and sorrows, and ultimately took our place on the cross. The verse goes on to say He was *"justified in the Spirit."* Although the exact phrase "in the spirit" isn't in the original Greek, the meaning is clear—Jesus was declared righteous by the Spirit, signifying His victory over sin and death. His resurrection wasn't just a return to life; it was a declaration of His righteousness and the validation of His sacrifice.

Peter adds another layer to this in 1 Peter 3:18, noting that Jesus was *"made alive in His spirit because He had become sin."* It's a reminder that His resurrection wasn't merely a physical event but a spiritual triumph. His spirit, which had taken on the sin of the world, was made alive, vindicated by the power of God. It's a powerful testament to the fact that everything Jesus did, He did for us. He took our place, bore our sins, and through His resurrection, offers us new life.

The death, burial, and resurrection of Jesus Christ are, without a doubt, the most important events in human history. They're not just stories from an ancient text; they're realities that have been verified by countless witnesses and supported by a wealth of evidence. The resurrection of Jesus isn't just a historical fact; it's a living truth that continues to impact lives today.

I find myself often coming back to that empty tomb, the place where hope was reborn. It's a reminder that no matter how dark the night, the dawn of resurrection is always just around the corner. Jesus' victory over death isn't just His victory; it's ours as well. His resurrection is the assurance that we, too, can overcome the grave, that we can rise above the struggles and trials of this life.

Reflecting on these events, I'm filled with a sense of awe and gratitude. Jesus' willingness to endure separation from the Father and to suffer a brutal death for my sake is a love story like no other. It's a story that invites me to live in the light of His resurrection, to embrace the new life He offers, and to walk in the hope that comes from knowing that death is not the end but the beginning of something beautiful and eternal.

As I ponder the magnitude of what Jesus accomplished through His death and resurrection, I am reminded that it's not just a story to be told but a truth to be lived. It's a call to embrace the life He offers, to walk in the freedom He secured, and to live each day with the hope and assurance that comes from knowing that because He lives, I, too, can face tomorrow.

Jesus' resurrection gives us the assurance that He is always with us, interceding on our behalf, guiding us, and preparing a place for us in His eternal kingdom. It is a reminder that no matter what trials or sufferings we face, there is a greater hope, a greater life waiting for us beyond the grave.

In light of His resurrection, I am called to live with a renewed sense of purpose and hope, knowing that my faith is rooted in the reality of a risen Savior who has conquered death and offers eternal life to all who believe. It is a call to live not just for this world, but for the eternal kingdom that awaits, a kingdom where death is no more and where we will dwell in the presence of our risen Lord forever.

HEAVEN

As I sit here, reflecting on the profound mystery of heaven, I am filled with a sense of awe and anticipation. The idea of Jesus ascending to heaven is not just a theological concept but a deeply personal and transformative reality. Heaven is described in Scripture with such beauty and grandeur that it stirs my soul and makes me long for that eternal home. I imagine what it must have been like for Jesus to ascend into the heavens, leaving behind the temporal to enter into the eternal, a place He has prepared for us.

The Bible paints a vivid picture of heaven, a place where the fullness of God's presence dwells. Psalm 80:14 talks about God's dwelling being in the heavens, and Isaiah 66:1 reminds us that heaven is His throne. These verses evoke an image of heaven as a place of ultimate authority and power, a reality that is both awe-inspiring and comforting. Jesus Himself spoke of heaven in Matthew 5:12, urging us to rejoice because our reward is great in heaven. I often think about Colossians 1:5, which speaks of the hope stored up for us in heaven, a hope that transcends our earthly struggles and pains.

HEAVEN

When I imagine heaven, I think of a place of unmatched beauty and splendor. Revelation 21:9-21 describes it as a place adorned with precious stones and pure gold, a city that shines with the glory of God. It's a place of bliss, as noted in Revelation 21:2, where the new Jerusalem descends from heaven, prepared like a bride for her husband. The imagery is deeply personal, speaking of a place prepared for those who are dearly loved. I am reminded of Jesus' words in John 14:1-3, where He promises that He is preparing a place for us, a place where we will dwell with Him forever. It is a place of joy and gladness, where every tear will be wiped away (Revelation 21:4), and where we will experience the fullness of satisfaction in His presence (Revelation 21:6-7).

One of the most striking descriptions of heaven is found in Revelation 21:23, where it is said that the city has no need for the sun or the moon because the glory of God illuminates it. The Lamb is its light, a reminder that heaven is a place of eternal light and glory. This resonates with the hope of a world free from darkness and sin, a place of perfect holiness as described in 2 Peter 3:13. As I think about the light of heaven, I am reminded of the times in my life when I have experienced moments of divine light, glimpses of that heavenly reality that awaits us.

Heaven is not just a place of splendor but also a place of fellowship and community. Revelation 21:9-10, 22-23 speaks of the bride, the Church, and the Lamb, Jesus Christ, dwelling together in perfect harmony. It's a place where we will be united with Christ, our Bridegroom, in an eternal relationship of love and intimacy. The thought of being in heaven with Jesus, along with all the saints and angelic beings (Isaiah 6:1-2; 2 Thessalonians 1:7; Revelation 3:5), fills me with anticipation and joy. I look forward to the day when we will join in the worship and adoration of our Creator alongside the angels, experiencing the fullness of His glory.

Heaven is often thought of as a place of rest, and Revelation 14:13 confirms that those who die in the Lord will rest from their labors. This rest is not about inactivity but about entering into a state of perfect peace and contentment, free from the burdens of this world. Revelation 5:14 describes a scene of worship in heaven, where all creatures bow down and worship God. I envision myself joining in that eternal chorus, lifting my voice in praise and adoration to the One who sits on the throne. Revelation 7:15 and 22:3 speak of service in heaven, where we will serve God day and night in His temple. This service is not out of obligation but out of a joyful response to His love and grace.

The most comforting thought about heaven is its eternal nature. Psalm 23:6 assures us that we will dwell in the house of the Lord forever, and 2 Corinthians 5:1 speaks of an eternal house in heaven, not built by human hands. Heaven is not a temporary respite but an eternal home where we will live in the presence of God forever. The idea of eternity is both awe-inspiring and humbling. It reminds me that our current life is just a fleeting moment compared to the eternity that awaits us in heaven.

As I reflect on these truths, I am filled with a deep sense of hope and longing for heaven. The thought of being in a place of beauty, joy, and eternal light, in the presence of Jesus and the saints, is something that gives me strength and encouragement in my daily walk. Heaven is not just a distant reality but a present hope that shapes how I live my life, reminding me that the best is yet to come.

Reflecting on the idea of heaven has always filled me with wonder and curiosity. The concept of heaven having different levels, each with its unique characteristics and purposes, offers a fascinating glimpse into the grandeur and complexity of God's creation. The Scriptures give us a profound understanding of these seven levels of heaven, revealing layers of divine order and purpose that stretch beyond our earthly comprehension.

HEAVEN

The first level, Vilon, as described in Isaiah 40:22, is a place where the work of creation is renewed daily. It's like the backdrop of the universe, a veil that encompasses everything we see and beyond. Every morning, I imagine God pulling back this veil to reveal a universe filled with new possibilities and endless wonder. It's incredible to think that the entire cosmos, beyond what our telescopes can observe, is being refreshed by the Creator's hand. This renewal reminds me that each day brings new mercies and opportunities to witness God's ongoing creative work.

The second level, Rakia, mentioned in Genesis 1:17, is the firmament where God set the sun, moon, and stars. This is the outer space, the vast expanse filled with galaxies, solar systems, and celestial bodies. When I gaze up at the night sky, I am in awe of the billions of stars scattered across the darkness, each one a testament to God's infinite creativity and power. It's humbling to think that we are just a tiny part of this immense and magnificent universe, carefully crafted and set in motion by the divine hand.

Shechakim, the third level, described in Psalm 78:23, is the atmosphere where manna was rained down for the Israelites. This level of heaven represents God's provision and sustenance. I imagine the sky opening up and pouring down blessings, just as it did with manna in the wilderness. It's a reminder that God provides for our needs in ways that are both miraculous and abundant. Every breath I take and every meal I enjoy is a reflection of the generosity that flows from this heavenly realm.

The fourth level, Zevul, is described in 1 Kings 8:13 and Isaiah 63:15 as a dwelling place. It's a level of heaven where the divine presence dwells, a place of profound significance and holiness. I think of this as a celestial home where the essence of God's presence is palpable and overwhelming. It's like a sanctuary where worship and communion with God are constant. This dwelling place reminds me that heaven is not just a distant concept but a home where we are meant to reside in the presence of our Creator.

Maon, the fifth level, mentioned in Psalm 42:8 and Deuteronomy 26:15, is where the ministering angels reside. This is a realm filled with heavenly beings who serve God and carry out His will. I imagine these angels as radiant and powerful, continually worshipping God and ministering to us on earth. Knowing that there is a level of heaven dedicated to these celestial servants gives me a sense of comfort and assurance that we are not alone in our spiritual journey. The angels are there, guiding and protecting us, working tirelessly to fulfill God's purposes.

The sixth level, Machon, described in Deuteronomy 28:12 and 1 Kings 8:39, is the location of the storehouses of heaven. This is where snow, rain, hail, and storms are kept. I envision this level as a vast, heavenly warehouse filled with the elements that sustain and shape our world. It's fascinating to think that the weather patterns and natural phenomena we experience are stored in a heavenly place, ready to be dispensed according to God's will. This reminds me of the power and majesty of God, who controls the forces of nature from His heavenly storehouses.

The seventh and highest level, Aravot, is described in Psalm 68:4 as the storehouse of life. This is where the seraphim dwell, the throne of glory is located, and where the King of the universe resides. This is the pinnacle of heaven, the ultimate realm of God's presence and authority. I imagine this level as a place of unimaginable beauty and light, where the glory of God shines brighter than any sun. It's a place where life in its purest form exists, where the angels and saints gather around the throne, singing praises to the King of Kings. This highest heaven represents the ultimate destination for those who are in Christ, a place where we will dwell in eternal joy and worship.

HEAVEN

The Apostle Paul, in 2 Corinthians 12:2, speaks of being caught up to the third heaven, a level of habitation where the divine presence is especially powerful. This populated level includes Zevul, Maon, and Aravot. These are the realms where the glory of God is most profoundly experienced, and where the angels and saints reside. Thinking about these levels of habitation fills me with a sense of awe and longing to be in that place where the fullness of God's presence is felt.

Reflecting on these seven levels of heaven, I am filled with a deep sense of wonder and anticipation. Each level reveals a different aspect of God's creation and His divine order. From the renewal of creation in Vilon to the highest heaven in Aravot, each realm speaks of a God who is infinitely creative, powerful, and loving. As I contemplate these heavenly realities, I am reminded that our journey on earth is just a prelude to an eternal adventure that awaits us in the presence of God. Heaven is not just a distant hope but a present reality that shapes how we live, worship, and serve.

Knowing that there are realms where angels dwell, where divine provision flows, and where the throne of glory stands, fills me with a sense of purpose and joy. It encourages me to live each day with the awareness that we are part of a much larger story, one that stretches beyond the stars and into the very heart of God's eternal kingdom.

When I first encountered the truth of justification through Christ, it felt like a veil lifting from my eyes, revealing a profound reality that reshaped everything I knew about God and myself. It wasn't just about a theological concept; it became a personal journey, a transformation that touched every corner of my existence.

Hebrews 1:1-6 reminds me of Jesus, the firstborn, whose resurrection sparked a new era. The moment Jesus rose from the dead, everything shifted. Acts 13:30-35 echoes this, highlighting God's declaration of righteousness over Jesus. "You are my Son; today I have begotten you," resonates deeply as God affirms Jesus, marking the defeat of Satan and stripping away hell's power. It was a spiritual rebirth, a cosmic reset.

Revelation 1:5-13 paints a majestic picture of Jesus as the firstborn from the dead, adorned with a golden breastplate. This imagery speaks of authority and victory, reminding me that Jesus not only conquered death but also holds ultimate power over all creation. Colossians 2:13-15 reinforces this victory, revealing how Jesus disarmed principalities and powers, triumphing over them publicly. His victory became our victory, transforming defeat into celebration.

Hebrews 2:14 describes how Jesus rendered the devil powerless, demolishing his works. The destruction of the devil's power means that pride, envy, jealousy, and sin no longer hold sway over those justified by faith in Christ (1 John 3:8). The once-insurmountable barrier of sin and death was shattered, as depicted in Matthew 27:51-53, where even death itself was defeated.

Reflecting on 1 Peter 3:18-19, I grasp the magnitude of Jesus' victory. He preached to the spirits in prison, not to offer salvation but to declare His triumph, making a spectacle of death itself. This act affirmed His authority over heaven, earth, and even beneath the earth. Ephesians 2:1-10 further illuminates this truth, revealing that in Christ's death and resurrection, we too were crucified, died, buried, justified, raised, and seated with Him in heavenly places. This profound identification with Christ reshapes our identity and purpose.

Colossians 2:11-14 seals this truth by depicting how God nailed our sins to the cross, wiping away the certificate of death that once stood against us. It was a declaration that the debt of sin had been paid in full, and through Christ, we were made new.

As I reflect on these truths, I realize that justification is not just a legal transaction but a personal invitation into a new life—a life where the power of sin is broken, where we are clothed in Christ's righteousness, and where we walk in the good works prepared for us. This journey of justification is ongoing, shaping me into the masterpiece God intended, empowered to live according to His plan from the very beginning.

In Christ, I find not only forgiveness but also transformation, not just freedom from sin but also empowerment to live victoriously. This is the story of justification—a story of grace, redemption, and a love that surpasses all understanding. It's a story I now live and share, for in Christ, I am justified, and in Him, I find my true identity and purpose.

As I sit here, reflecting on the concept of heaven and the seven levels that stretch across the divine realms, I can't help but feel a profound sense of awe and anticipation. It's not just an abstract idea or a distant dream; it's a real, tangible place that promises beauty, joy, and eternal fulfillment. The thought of heaven being layered with different levels, each with its unique purpose and wonder, fills me with a sense of excitement and curiosity about what lies beyond our earthly existence.

In Revelation, we see heaven as a city of gold, with gates of pearl and streets of pure, transparent glass. It's a place where the light of God illuminates everything, where there is no need for sun or moon because His glory is all-encompassing. This vision of heaven fills me with hope and longing, a desire to be in that place where everything is made new, where we will dwell with God and experience the fullness of His love and grace.

As I ponder these things, I am reminded that our time on earth is but a fleeting moment compared to the eternity that awaits us. Heaven is not just our final destination; it is our true home, the place where we were always meant to be. It's where we will find rest from our labors, where we will worship God in the fullness of His presence, and where we will serve Him with joy and gladness forever.

Thinking about heaven changes the way I live my life here and now. It gives me perspective, reminding me that the trials and struggles of this world are temporary and that there is something far greater waiting for me on the other side. It inspires me to live with purpose, to love deeply, and to seek after God with all my heart. Knowing that heaven is my final destination fills me with a sense of peace and anticipation, a hope that anchors my soul and gives me strength for each day.

In the end, the promise of heaven is not just about the future; it's about living each day with the hope and assurance that we are on a journey to a place where all things are made right, where love and joy abound, and where we will be with our Creator forever. Heaven is for real, and it's our ultimate home, a place of unimaginable beauty and eternal joy. As I continue on this journey, I hold on to the hope of heaven, looking forward to the day when I will see my Savior face to face and dwell in His presence forever.

May this hope of heaven fill your heart with peace and inspire you to live each day with the assurance that our final destination is a place of eternal joy and rest in the presence of God.

HEAVEN

THE COMMISSION

When I first encountered Christ's commission, it was like a sudden gust of wind on a still summer day—unexpected yet undeniably transformative. Growing up, I had heard about Jesus in passing, seen His name on church signs, and caught glimpses of His story in the occasional Bible verse. But it wasn't until I experienced a personal encounter with His commission that everything changed.

Christ's commission, as outlined in Matthew 28:19-20, resonates deeply with me. Those words, "*Go therefore and make disciples of all nations, baptizing them in the name of the Father and of the Son and of the Holy Spirit, teaching them to observe all that I have commanded you*," are not just instructions; they are a calling that beckons me into a journey of faith and obedience.

Reflecting on the original commission given by Jesus to His disciples, I am reminded of the weight of those words. Imagine standing on that mountain, looking into the eyes of the resurrected Christ, feeling the gravity of His charge to spread the gospel to the ends of the earth. It was a mission that transcended time and culture, a mission that spoke to

THE COMMISSION

the heart of humanity's deepest need for salvation and reconciliation with God.

For me, embracing Christ's commission wasn't a single moment but a series of moments—a gradual awakening to the significance of sharing the love and truth of Jesus with others. It started with small steps: a timid invitation to church, a hesitant conversation about faith, a prayer for someone in need. Each step was a response to Christ's call to go and make disciples, to share His love in tangible ways.

In Acts 1:8, Jesus promises His disciples that they will receive power when the Holy Spirit comes upon them, enabling them to be witnesses in Jerusalem, Judea, Samaria, and to the ends of the earth. This promise extends to us today, empowering us to fulfill Christ's commission with boldness and conviction. It's not about our abilities or qualifications but about God's Spirit working through us to accomplish His purposes.

As I journey in obedience to Christ's commission, I am continually reminded of the profound impact of His love and grace in my own life. Just as Jesus met me in my brokenness and showed me the way to redemption, I now have the privilege and responsibility to share that same message of hope with others. This commission is not just a task to check off a list; it's a calling to participate in God's redemptive work in the world.

In this journey of embracing Christ's commission, I have discovered a deeper sense of purpose and fulfillment. It's not always easy, and there are moments of doubt and fear. Yet, in those moments, I cling to the assurance that God is faithful and His commission is worth every sacrifice and every step of faith. It's a journey of learning to trust God more deeply, to rely on His strength rather than my own, and to surrender to His leading in every aspect of my life.

JESUS: MY ROLE MODEL

When I first encountered Mark 16:15-18 and Jesus' clear command to His disciples, it struck me with a profound sense of both responsibility and promise. Jesus didn't mince words when He instructed His followers to "*go into all the world and preach the good news to all creation.*" This wasn't just a suggestion; it was a commission—an urgent call to share the life-transforming message of the Gospel with everyone, everywhere.

What resonated deeply with me was not only the command to preach but also the assurance that accompanied it: "*Whoever believes and is baptized will be saved.*" Salvation—the ultimate reconciliation with God—was offered freely to all who would believe in Jesus. But Jesus didn't stop there; He made a promise that resonates powerfully even today: "And these signs will accompany those who believe..."

Jesus listed miraculous signs that would follow believers: driving out demons, speaking in new tongues, handling snakes, drinking poison without harm, and healing the sick by laying hands on them. These were not just random acts of power but demonstrations of God's authority over every realm—spiritual, physical, and even natural. It was a declaration that the Kingdom of God was breaking into the world, bringing freedom, restoration, and wholeness.

As I pondered these words, I couldn't help but confront the common misconceptions that surround healing in today's theology. Jesus didn't add disclaimers like "*if it is my will*" or "*unless suffering is necessary for spiritual growth.*" No, He unequivocally declared, "*They will get well.*" This promise wasn't conditional upon circumstances or explanations; it was a straightforward assurance of God's desire and power to bring healing.

Reflecting on scriptures like James 5:14-15, which instructs believers to call the elders to pray over the sick and anoint them with oil in the name of the Lord, reinforces this truth. The prayer offered in faith will save the sick, and the Lord will raise them up. This aligns perfectly with Jesus' commission in Mark 16—to proclaim the Gospel and demonstrate its power through signs and wonders.

I realized that healing is not merely a sidebar to the Gospel but an integral part of it. It's a tangible expression of God's love and mercy, a demonstration of His Kingdom come on earth as it is in heaven. This revelation reshaped my understanding of God's will: if He commands us to proclaim healing, it must be His will for everyone to experience His wholeness and restoration.

In my own journey of faith, I've witnessed moments where God's healing power broke through in miraculous ways. I've seen illnesses vanish, bodies restored, and lives transformed. These experiences affirmed Jesus' words in Mark 16—they underscored the reality that God's desire to heal extends to every person, regardless of circumstance or background.

Moreover, I've learned that embracing the promise of healing isn't just about experiencing physical restoration; it's about encountering the heart of a God who cares intimately for His creation. It's about stepping into the authority given to us as believers, boldly declaring God's promises, and trusting His sovereignty over every situation.

When I first encountered Christ's promise in Mark 16:18, declaring, *"They will place their hands on the sick, and they will get well,"* it struck me with a simplicity and power that challenged my understanding of God's will for healing. Jesus didn't hedge His words or make exceptions; He spoke directly to His disciples and by extension, to all believers throughout history, including me. This promise wasn't reserved for a select few; it was for anyone who believes in Him. That realization changed everything for me.

The clarity of Christ's words brought to mind His broader promise of salvation: *"Whoever believes... will be saved."* This principle applies universally to all sinners who turn to Him in faith. It's a sweeping assurance of God's inclusive love and grace—no one is excluded from the opportunity to receive forgiveness and eternal life through Jesus Christ. Similarly, Jesus extends this inclusivity to physical healing—there are no exceptions. If we believe, healing is part of the package.

Reflecting on the example of the Early Church in Acts 5:16, I saw how they embraced Jesus' teachings and promises wholeheartedly. They believed in miracles and prayed with expectation, knowing that God's power was not limited by circumstances or diagnoses. The crowds gathered, bringing their sick and those tormented by evil spirits, and the Scriptures declare that ALL of them were healed. This wasn't just a one-time event but a pattern of faith and expectation that characterized the early believers.

The disciples themselves witnessed Jesus' ministry firsthand and never saw Him turn away anyone who came to Him for healing. He met each person with compassion and authority, demonstrating God's desire to bring wholeness to every aspect of their lives. They learned directly from His example and teachings, understanding that healing was not just a physical act but a manifestation of God's Kingdom breaking into the world.

Paul's teaching in Galatians 3:13 reinforced this truth for me. He boldly declared that Christ redeemed us from the curse of the Law by becoming a curse for us. This redemption isn't partial; it's comprehensive—covering every area where sin and brokenness have touched our lives, including sickness and disease. As believers, we are beneficiaries of this redemption, standing in the freedom and authority that Christ secured for us on the cross.

Embracing the promise of healing isn't about denying the reality of illness or minimizing medical wisdom. It's about aligning our faith with God's Word and His promises. It's about stepping out in confidence, knowing that God desires to bring His healing touch into our lives and the lives of those around us. It's about praying with expectation, believing that God's power is as real and effective today as it was in the days of the Early Church.

In my own journey, I've experienced moments where God's healing power has been evident. I've seen prayers answered, bodies restored, and lives transformed by His miraculous touch. These experiences have deepened my faith and solidified my conviction that God's promises are true and reliable. They've taught me to pray boldly, to trust in His timing, and to never doubt His willingness to bring healing according to His perfect will.

When I first encountered Paul's teachings about Christ taking our place and redeeming us from the curses of the Law, it felt like a revelation unfolding before me. Paul's Gospel wasn't just about forgiveness of sins—it encompassed healing for all believers. This truth resonated deeply with me because it shattered the misconception that healing might be selective or conditional. Christ suffered all the curses of the Law on our behalf, making no exceptions. This meant that His redemptive work on the cross included not only spiritual restoration but also physical healing for those who believe.

James' straightforward question in his epistle challenged me: "*Is any of you sick?*" His answer was equally direct and comforting: "*The prayer offered in faith will make the sick person well; the Lord will raise him up*" (James 5:15, paraphrased). The Greek word "*sozo*," used here for "*will make well*," underscores James' belief that healing and forgiveness are inseparable components of the Gospel. This promise is inclusive—it applies to all believers, regardless of their circumstances or past mistakes. Just as it did in the Early Church, this promise stands true today.

John's perspective in 1 John 5:14 further affirmed God's willingness to hear and respond to our prayers, especially when they align with His will. John wrote, "*This is the confidence we have in approaching God: that if we ask anything according to his will, he hears us.*" The key

JESUS: MY ROLE MODEL

phrase, *"according to his will,"* emphasizes that God's will is revealed through His Word and His promises. When we pray for healing, we can do so with confidence, knowing that it aligns with God's desire to bring wholeness and restoration to His people.

Reflecting on John's words, I realized that "anything" in prayer includes healing. It's not a presumptuous request but a bold declaration of faith in God's character and His promises. As one of Jesus' closest disciples, John understood firsthand Christ's ministry of healing. He witnessed Jesus' compassion and power as He touched the lives of countless individuals, bringing healing and restoration wherever He went. John's confidence in God's will for healing stemmed from these experiences and the teachings of Jesus Himself.

When I first began to understand the depth of the Gospel's promise of healing, it felt like discovering a hidden treasure that had always been right in front of me. John's Gospel makes it clear: healing is not just an optional extra, but an integral part of the message of Jesus Christ. This truth was both liberating and empowering, challenging the limitations I had placed on God's willingness and ability to heal.

The apostle Peter's words in 1 Peter 2:24 resonated deeply with me: *"By whose wounds you have been healed."* This isn't a vague or conditional statement; it's a definitive promise. The word "you" encompasses all believers—every single person who places their faith in Jesus Christ. There are no exceptions. Peter's declaration is a direct invitation to receive healing for all sicknesses including mental and psychological, rooted in the sacrificial wounds of Christ. It was a reminder that Jesus' suffering was not just for the forgiveness of sins but also for the healing of our bodies.

Reflecting on Paul's ministry, I was struck by his uncompromising proclamation of the Gospel. In Acts 20:20, Paul boldly declared, *"I have not hesitated to preach anything that would be helpful to you."* Healing, undeniably, falls into the category of what is helpful, especially for those

THE COMMISSION

who are sick. Paul's Gospel was comprehensive; it included not only spiritual redemption but also physical restoration. His unwavering commitment to this message was evident throughout his missionary journeys, where healing was a common and expected part of his ministry.

One story that stands out vividly is Paul's time on the island of Malta. As recorded in Acts 28:8-9, Paul encountered the chief official's father, who was bedridden with fever and dysentery. Paul didn't hesitate; he prayed, laid hands on the man, and healed him. This act of compassion and faith sparked a wave of healing across the island, as "the rest of the sick on the island came and were cured." There were no exceptions; everyone who sought healing received it. This wasn't just a historical account—it was a testament to the unchanging nature of God's healing power and the inclusive scope of His love.

As I pondered these accounts, I couldn't help but notice the stark contrast between the miraculous, faith-filled beginnings of the Early Church and the often lukewarm approach of modern Christianity. The Early Church was characterized by a fervent belief in miracles and a readiness to act on Jesus' command to heal the sick. They didn't just preach about healing; they practiced it with boldness and expectancy. Their faith in action brought about tangible results, demonstrating the Kingdom of God in real and powerful ways.

In today's world, it seems that the fire of that early faith has dimmed in many places. The Church, in some circles, has become hesitant to embrace the full scope of the Gospel, often relegating healing to a footnote rather than a foundational promise. This lukewarm approach contrasts sharply with the vibrant faith of the Early Church, which saw healing as an essential part of their mission and witness.

For me, this realization sparked a desire to return to the "Bible Way"—to reclaim the fullness of the Gospel that includes healing for all. It's a call to move away from a watered-down version of Christianity and embrace the robust, life-transforming message of Jesus Christ. This means not only preaching about healing but also stepping out in faith to pray for the sick, believing that God's promise to heal is as relevant today as it was in the days of the apostles.

We are called to follow the example of the Early Church, not just in their teachings but in their actions. When we do, we can expect to see the same kind of miraculous results they experienced. The Gospel of the Lord Jesus Christ is a Gospel of hope, redemption, and healing for all who believe. It's a message that has the power to transform lives, heal the sick, and bring the light of God's love to a hurting world.

When I first dove into the writings of Paul, I was struck by how deeply he intertwined the message of the Gospel with demonstrations of God's power. It wasn't enough for him to simply speak about Christ; he insisted that his words be confirmed by tangible acts of the Spirit. Paul's approach to proclaiming the Gospel wasn't just about delivering an eloquent speech or a compelling argument; it was about showcasing the very power of God at work in real, undeniable ways.

In Romans 15:18-19, Paul clearly articulated this perspective: "*I will not venture to speak of anything except what Christ has accomplished through me in leading the Gentiles to obey God by what I have said and done—by the power of signs and miracles, through the power of the Spirit.*" This passage paints a vivid picture of a man who viewed his mission as incomplete without the supernatural. From Jerusalem to Illyricum, Paul's ministry was marked by signs, wonders, and miracles. For him, this was the full proclamation of the Gospel—a message that was not only heard but also seen and felt.

Reflecting on this, I realized how often we, in modern times, might separate the Gospel into mere words, stripping it of the power that is supposed to accompany it. We might deliver a powerful sermon or engage in thoughtful debate, but how often do we expect God to show up in miraculous ways, confirming His message with undeniable acts of

THE COMMISSION

His Spirit? Paul's ministry challenges us to expect more—to anticipate that God will back up His Word with His power.

The Early Church understood this well. They preached Christ's message, and their preaching was validated by healings and the casting out of demons in Jesus' Name. This wasn't an occasional occurrence but a regular part of their ministry. Acts records numerous instances where the apostles preached, and miracles followed, leading many to faith in Christ. Imagine if a preacher today claimed to deliver the Gospel but showed no evidence of God's power. In the context of the Early Church, such a person would likely be dismissed as inauthentic. Their message came "not simply with words, but also with power, with the Holy Spirit and with deep conviction" (1 Thessalonians 1:5).

Paul's own words in 1 Corinthians 2:1-5 further emphasize this point: "*My message and my preaching were not with wise and persuasive words, but with a demonstration of the Spirit's power, so that your faith might not rest on human wisdom, but on God's power.*" This is a profound reminder that the Gospel is not about human eloquence or intellectual prowess; it's about the transformative power of God. It's about faith that is grounded in the reality of God's presence and action, not just in theoretical or philosophical concepts.

One of my most vivid memories of experiencing this power was during a mission trip. We were in a remote village in India, and the need for healing was overwhelming. The people were suffering from various ailments, and the local healthcare resources were scarce. We preached the Gospel, but we also prayed fervently for healing. As we prayed, we witnessed God's miraculous power at work—people were healed, and their faith was ignited in ways that words alone could never accomplish. It was a clear demonstration that "*the kingdom of God is not a matter of talk but of power*" (1 Corinthians 4:20).

This experience reinforced in me the truth that the Gospel is a living, dynamic force. It's not just a set of doctrines to be discussed or debated;

it's the power of God for salvation and transformation. This power isn't confined to the pages of Scripture or the history of the Early Church; it's available to us today. The same God who worked through Paul and the apostles is at work in our world, and He desires to confirm His Word with signs, wonders, and miracles.

As I continue to grow in my faith, I am reminded that the full Gospel—Paul's Gospel—is one that cannot be separated from the demonstration of God's power. It challenges me to preach and live out my faith in a way that expects and welcomes the supernatural. It's a call to step beyond the confines of comfortable religiosity and into the vibrant, life-changing reality of God's Kingdom here on earth. May we all embrace this full Gospel, boldly proclaiming and demonstrating the power of God in our lives and in the world around us.

THE COMMISSION

CONCLUSION

As I conclude this book, the story of Jesus is no not just a collection of ancient tales but a living testimony that speaks to me personally, teaching me, guiding me, and transforming me. Jesus, in His profound humanity and divine mission, stands as the ultimate role model and friend—a beacon of hope, love, and purpose.

When I think about Jesus, I see not just a distant figure of worship, but a friend who walks beside me in every season of life. His compassion, kindness, and unwavering support make Him the kind of friend we all long for. He laughed with His disciples, shared meals with outcasts, and wept with those who mourned. In moments of loneliness or doubt, I find comfort in knowing that Jesus understands, because He, too, experienced the full range of human emotions. He is the friend who is always there, offering a listening ear and a comforting presence.

Jesus' life wasn't just a series of random acts of kindness; it was part of a grand, divine plan orchestrated by God. From His humble birth in a manger to His triumphant resurrection, every step He took was purposeful and intentional. This master plan reminds me that my life, too, is part of something bigger than myself. When I face challenges or

CONCLUSION

uncertainty, I remember that God has a plan for me, just as He had for Jesus. It's a plan for good, to give me a future and a hope.

At the heart of Jesus' mission was His role as Saviour. He came not just to teach or heal, but to offer Himself as a sacrifice for my sins. On the cross, He bore the weight of my shortcomings, my failures, my brokenness. It's a humbling thought that the Son of God would endure such suffering out of love for me. His death and resurrection offer me forgiveness and new life, a chance to start over and to live in the freedom that comes from being redeemed.

The incarnation, the astounding truth that God clothed Himself in flesh, is a mystery that fills me with awe. Jesus, fully God and fully man, walked among us, experiencing life as we do. He knew hunger, thirst, fatigue, and joy. In Jesus, I see the perfect balance of divinity and humanity—a God who is not distant or detached, but intimately involved in the human experience. His life on earth is a reminder that God understands my struggles and walks with me through every challenge.

Reflecting on the humanity of Jesus, I am struck by His vulnerability and empathy. He faced temptations, felt sorrow, and experienced pain. In the Garden of Gethsemane, He prayed with such intensity that His sweat was like drops of blood. He understands my weaknesses and fears because He faced them Himself. Jesus' humanity assures me that it's okay to be human, to struggle, and to seek God's strength in my moments of weakness.

Jesus' journey to the cross was marked by immense suffering and sacrifice. Betrayed by a friend, tried unjustly, and crucified between thieves, He endured it all out of love for me. The cross is not just a symbol of suffering; it's a testament to the depth of God's love. Jesus' sacrifice on the cross paid the price for my sins, offering me forgiveness and reconciliation with God. It's a powerful reminder that I am deeply loved and that my life has immense value.

JESUS: MY ROLE MODEL

What Jesus did on the cross was not the end of the story. He descended into Hell, conquering death and sin, and rose victoriously on the third day. His resurrection is a declaration of victory, a promise that death is not the end but the beginning of eternal life. It's a victory that I can share in, a hope that gives me courage and strength to face life's challenges.

Jesus' resurrection opens the door to the hope of heaven—a place of beauty, joy, and eternal peace. It's a promise of a future where there is no more pain, no more sorrow, and no more death. Heaven is real, and it's my final destination, a place where I will be with Jesus forever. This hope fills me with joy and anticipation, knowing that the best is yet to come.

Before ascending to heaven, Jesus gave a commission to go into all the world and share the good news. It's a call to action, a reminder that my life has a purpose beyond myself. I am called to be a witness to His love, to share His message of hope and salvation with others. It's a mission that gives my life meaning and direction, a mission that I am honored to be part of.

In every aspect of His life, Jesus is my role model. His love, compassion, humility, and courage inspire me to live a life that reflects His character. He shows me what it means to love selflessly, to serve others, and to walk in faith. As I strive to follow His example, I am transformed into His likeness, becoming a beacon of His love in a world that desperately needs it.

The life of Jesus is a story of love, sacrifice, and hope. It's a story that I am privileged to be part of, a story that transforms my life and gives me a purpose. Jesus, in His humanity and divinity, is the ultimate role model and friend. He shows me the way to live, to love, and to hope. As I reflect on His life and teachings, I am inspired to follow Him more closely, to share His love with others, and to live a life that honors Him. Jesus is not just a historical figure; He is my Savior, my friend,

CONCLUSION

and my role model, guiding me on the journey of faith and leading me to the hope of eternal life with Him.

THE END!